D0500124

GIFTS

OF AN EAGLE

Kent Durden

KENDALL/HUNT PUBLISHING COMPANY
4050 Westmark Drive   Dubuque, Iowa 52002

To My Mother
who for so many years
shared her husband with an eagle

Contents

Lady Comes to Live With Us	7
Early Training	13
Adolescent Years	23
A Relationship Grows	35
Filling the Larder	45
Eagle Sense	61
Motherhood	73
A New Home	91
Bit Parts	103
A Feature Role	125
Mature Years	141
A Courtship in the Air	151
Epilogue	157

LADY COMES
TO LIVE WITH US

Many true stories have been written describing the relationships between man and the various members of the animal kingdom that have become his devoted and loved pets. Few true stories record a relationship lasting as long as this one, and even fewer involve a creature as proud and noble as a golden eagle. This, then, is the story of "Lady," who for sixteen years shared her life with a human family and gave her devoted loyalty to her master.

It is difficult for me to recall a time in my life when Lady wasn't part of the family. There are faint recollections of that brilliant spring day in 1954 when my father and I inched our way down a steep cliff, carefully lowering ourselves to a point just above a huge pile of sticks. Clinging to scrub oaks and manzanitas, we made the decision to take the final step and capture the huge nestling golden eagle that we knew rested quietly against the cliff just beneath us.

For several years we had entertained the thought of training a golden eagle for falconry. Together Dad and I had

7

trained many hawks and falcons, and often while flying our hawks, we would see eagles in flight. We would gaze in awe at their huge size, and the thought of being able to cause an eagle to plunge from the sky at our beck and call haunted us day and night.

At that time the golden eagle was a state-protected bird —now they are federally protected—and, as such, they belonged to the People of California. In order to legally retain an eagle in captivity, we had to obtain a permit from the State Department of Fish and Game. We were thrilled when we finally received the permit. It stated that we were obtaining the eagle for "educational and research purposes," to increase the public's knowledge of the golden eagle. Also in the fine print it stated bluntly that our permit could be revoked at any time "without cause or reason."

Now the search for an eagle's nest was begun in earnest. Dad took to the air in his small plane and began to search the country for adult eagles. It wasn't long before he spotted a pair of adult eagles soaring high over the Conejo Valley to the east of our home in Carpinteria. He joined the big birds for a while as they circled in the thermals. They seemed not to mind the company of the large red and white "bird," and he often passed within a hundred feet of them without causing alarm. Then he drifted away and began a thorough search of the cliffs on the mountains around the valley. In less than an hour he covered more cliffs than a man could explore on foot in a week. At last he spotted the telltale sign; a ledge with a jumbled pile of sticks streaked with the whitewashing of years of use. He swung closer on the next pass, and as he glided by, got a glimpse of the downy nestling lying quietly in the cup of the nest, waiting for the return of its parents. The chick raised itself up to look at the big "bird" passing by. Dad eased the throttle open and headed for home. He planned to return from time to time to check on the size of the young bird. It was important to let the old birds feed it for as long as possible.

The training of the golden eagle was not our only goal in getting the bird. We wanted to study the intelligence and behavior of the king of birds and, above all, we wanted to record the entire story on motion-picture film. The first chapter of our film would be the training of the golden eagle.

By capturing the nestling, we knew, we were accepting the responsibility for her welfare and safety, not a thing to take lightly. I fastened the rope and held it taut as Dad made his way over the edge. It was three hundred feet to the bottom, and I kept a cautious eye on the oak that held the lifeline. I heard a low whistle as Dad got his first close view of the object of our efforts. The eagle was a nestling in name only. By her size one wouldn't classify her as a helpless infant, as the word nestling implies. She stood almost two feet high and was almost completely feathered out, with only a few downy tufts remaining around her head.

She made her defense at the back of the ledge, facing her enemy with gaping mouth and extended talons. A considerable time passed as Dad and the eagle eyed each other. Dad knew that he had to get her by the ankles, just above the large talons, before she had a chance to use her weapons. There wasn't much room to move about on the ledge, the nest being about six feet wide and four feet deep. Made up entirely of sticks and twigs piled one upon another, it represented several years of nesting activity. Every movement by Dad sent a tremor through the wobbly pile and reminded him of the three-hundred-foot drop to the valley floor.

As he eased toward the bird, she pressed her back against the cliff and stared wildly at his face. He carefully selected his precise target and with lightning speed grabbed the bird's ankles. In an instant she was thrashing all around the nest, causing the whole pile to wobble threateningly. With great difficulty he finally succeeded in putting her into a gunnysack and tying a rope to it. The signal was given, and I began to pull the sack up the cliff.

As the sack came into view, I was eager for my first glimpse of the bird who would become a part of our lives. Looking back in retrospect now, it is no surprise that the first parts of the eagle's anatomy to greet me were eight long, black, curved sabers protruding through the burlap like some medieval torture trap just waiting to be sprung. A good part of my life would be spent dodging the swift movements of those taloned feet.

On the ride home, Dad and I talked casually about the future days of training, trying to hide our feelings of anxiety about taking on such a project; meanwhile the eagle lay in her darkened sack at our side, her huge talons clenched in quiet determination.

The large cage with heavy fishnet sides had been prepared and waiting for weeks in anticipation of our honored guest. We entered with the sack and carefully though unceremoniously spilled the jumbled mass of black feathers, talons, and yellow feet out onto the dirt floor. For a moment the mass of feathers weaved about somewhat unsteadily as the great bird adjusted itself to this abrupt change. Then the feathers began to take on form and shape as the eagle arranged her wing and tail feathers and gathered her feet beneath her. Only then did we begin to realize just how large this bird was. She was magnificent! When standing erect she was almost two feet tall. Her sturdy legs were about one inch in diameter at the ankle, and at the thighs about two inches. Feathers covered the legs all the way to the feet. The thick yellow feet were armed with eight curved black talons from one to three inches long. The broad chest gave indications of the strong pectoral muscles needed to drive the seven-foot wings.

There is probably no more fierce face than that of a wild eagle. The yellow-brown eyes are set at a forward angle, each protected by a boney, feathered shield called a superorbital bone. This gives the bird a perpetual look of fierceness. The ebony bill adds to the total effect with its wicked hook designed for tearing flesh to shreds.

At this point in our observations, the eagle became aware of our presence. She wasted no time in coming to the conclusion that we were the cause of all her troubles. As she turned to face us, we realized that this was no ordinary bird. Most birds of prey when first captured will retreat backward until they are cornered, and then put up a fight, or they will simply try to flee. But here before us this golden eagle ignored the drive to flee and instead attacked us! In our haste to retreat we stumbled over one another until we had gained the safety of the outside.

After she had cleared the cage of unwanted occupants, she surveyed the surroundings. It was a large cage, about twenty feet long and eight feet wide, with sides of fishnetting. An alcove provided a darker place for a resting area. We watched as she walked around the cage in her heavy, swaggering stride. Then she looked up at the perch we had so carefully prepared with soft leather padding fastened with shiny brass tacks; it provided, we thought, a seat fitting for the queen of birds.

To our delight she hopped up on it. But then a look of contempt came over her as she examined the soft perch. Suddenly she began to tear and rip the leather with her powerful bill, casting each piece disdainfully over her shoulder until our beautiful perch was in shreds, and her yellow feet rested firmly and somewhat proudly on the rough bare wood. She had just demonstrated to us that, although she was our captive, she was still able to exercise certain prerogatives of her own, even if it was only in selecting the type of perch to rest on.

From this first experience we began to realize just a bit of the proud and aggressive nature of this great bird. We had much more to learn. To the surprise of everyone, we named her Lady. Not "lady" as a delicate member of the weaker sex (which she certainly did not typify) but "Lady" as a proud, regal member of the nobility. We retreated to the house to plan our strategy for the next day.

EARLY TRAINING

Before one can train any bird of prey, a leash must be attached to the bird. Obviously a collar can't be put on the neck, so short leather straps are fastened to each ankle by the use of an ancient knot known as the falconer's knot. These short leather straps are called jesses. To the two jesses a single leather leash is attached by the use of a snap hook. The attachment of the jesses was the first step in the training of this eagle.

I do not remember how we ever managed to get the jesses fastened to Lady's feet. However, I can remember ten pounds of thrashing, screaming eagle. Since this was the first step in the training, we had the cameras rolling for the event. It was our belief that the eagle wouldn't use her bill in defense, and since I had her feet firmly in my grasp, we felt quite safe. But our theory was quickly shattered. The film shows very clearly how Lady scored a bullseye on my nose with her hooked beak.

With the jesses firmly attached, we again returned her to

the cage. She was still a young bird and we didn't want to risk injuring her limbs by allowing her to struggle against the jesses and leash. We needed time also to get her accustomed to our presence before proceeding further. We began by working with her in the dark of night. Most birds of prey are helpless and refuse to move if they can't see. There are two ways of achieving this condition. One way is using an artificial device called a hood, which is simply a fashioned leather cap that slips over the head of the bird, thus blinding it. The other way to achieve blindness is to simply work with the bird in the darkness of night.

For many nights Dad worked with Lady. Standing next to her in the darkness, he would talk softly and stroke her feathers gently with his hand. At first she flinched when he spoke, but then gradually she became accustomed to his voice. This went on night after night. Gradually Dad introduced the gloved hand by touching the back of her legs. Before long she was standing on his gloved arm, while he stroked her with his other hand and talked to her in soothing tones. Little by little, in the black of night, the unique relationship between my father and Lady was established, a bond between man and bird that was to last for sixteen years.

Although Lady seemed tame at night, the days were another matter. As we approached the cage, she would stand at the far perch eyeing us closely, first with one eye and then with the other, looking deceptively gentle. Upon our entry into her cage she would attack us. We tried to avoid any unnecessary movements. We merely wanted her to allow us to stand in her presence. This she flatly refused. We were well prepared, with legs well padded and with leather jackets and heavy gloves and at times even a fencing mask. Lady would aim about chest-high, flying at full force from about fifteen feet away. Always we managed to throw up an arm

14

for her to contact. She would slam into it with both taloned feet, give it a couple of bone-crushing squeezes, and then drop to the ground, where she rebounded instantly at our knees. This attack would be met by gloved fist held just at the level of her sturdy breast. Time and again she would rebound, almost like a punching bag, to the fist. Finally, exhausted, she would return to her perch. Any sudden movement on our part as we left the cage would very likely trigger another attack.

Frightening as these attacks were, they provided us with very important information about Lady's strength and endurance. Even though her bones were still young and her muscles still developing, she possessed fantastic strength in her feet. We realized that this bird could easily kill a man if her talons ever found the right mark. However, we had to continue our efforts each day until she would allow us to enter her cage.

It was two weeks before Lady would allow us to enter her little domain without attack. Even when she did, she was very definitely in control of the situation. If we moved too quickly or did something she didn't approve of, she would threaten us by various means which we always recognized. Progress at this point was very slow, but gradually, through day-to-day contact, we were able to stand next to her and finally touch her.

We now had an eagle who would give us permission to stand in her presence and, of all things, touch her! Now we had to train her to ride on the gloved arm. This is the only way to transport a bird of prey. Such birds cannot be carried in the arms like a cat, nor can they be led on a leash like a dog. The heavy glove serves two purposes. First, it is a protection from the talons; second, it provides the bird with a steadier perch to grip. It would be impossible for an eagle to maintain her balance on an ungloved arm due to the looseness of the flesh.

To our surprise, Lady learned to step on the gloved arm quite easily. However, she could hop off any time she pleased since we were still in the cage. The day soon came to take her outside for the first time. For this we had to attach the leash to the jesses. Until this time she had been able to move about at will within the confines of the cage. Now for the first time she had to remain on the fist against her will. She tried to fly off immediately. This movement is called bating; it involves probably the most strenuous activity of the training for both bird and trainer. As the bird launches from the fist, the trainer keeps the jesses tight so the bird is swung down to hang upside down until the trainer with the other hand swings it back up on the fist. Often in the early stages the bird will refuse to grip the glove and will fall off again and again. With a bird as heavy as a golden eagle, the trainer's arm soon wearies. Consequently, these lessons are of short duration. Many days passed before Lady finally realized she couldn't get off and became "made" to the fist. She finally became so accustomed to this manner of transportation that she preferred the fist to a stationary perch. Through all these steps Dad filmed as I proceeded with the training. The film was to portray how to train a young eagle, and in the film I was the trainer, a boy of sixteen. In reality, it was Dad who first introduced Lady to each new stage of training. He had her trust and respect. Once she was moderately accustomed to the new step, I began to work with her while Dad filmed. In this way I benefited from the trust and respect she had for him. Although Lady would perform for me obediently, as she was trained to do, it was only because Dad had first spent much time with her. We began to notice very early that she resented my intrusions upon the scene. She tolerated me, but only very reluctantly.

These early days were filled with many crises as we progressed through each stage of training. Lady resented very strongly any variations in her regular routine. The time came to begin flight training to the fist. The motivation for her to fly to the fist was food. Properly trained, she could be called from hundreds of feet in the air back to the fist. This is the only way a trainer can retrieve the bird in the field. Up until this time, Lady had been fed her meals in her cage from Dad's or my fist where she usually consumed her entire meal of raw meat. She always willingly accepted food from our hands, so it must have been a great surprise to her one day when we held the food about fifteen inches away from her. She couldn't reach it without jumping the few inches. This distance was the first step in what we hoped would finally be extended to several hundred feet. However, our aspirations were cooled when she flatly refused to take this first step. The offering was withdrawn, and two hours later it was made again. Again it was refused. She didn't eat that afternoon.

The next morning the process was repeated with the same results. Again, the third day. We began to wonder if she would ever submit to our demands. Was her will so strong that she could refuse this critical step in training? Each time, as we approached with food, her hunger was obvious. Eagerly she eyed the meat, but when we held it at a distance, thus forcing her to come to us, her eagerness was replaced by her determination not to yield to our demands. Standing rigidly, she would try desperately to ignore the food.

On the morning of the fourth day, I again approached her on the outdoor perch. Dad was away for the day and had left me instructions to continue offering her meat every two hours. This time her expression was different. There

17

was a wild look about her that I tried to ignore as I extended my gloved arm with the tempting piece of horsemeat. Her taloned feet were planted firmly on the perch, her feathers were tightly compressed. As she eyed the meat, a twittering began deep in her throat. It was a sound one would not expect from so large a bird, almost a canary sound. The twittering began to rise in volume and frequency as Lady began to sway back and forth like an athlete with feet firmly anchored as he is about to hurl the discus. With each sway toward me she lowered her head menacingly and raised the feathers along the back of her neck. I stood my ground, not because of bravery, but because I was transfixed by the sight. Suddenly she uncoiled like a spring, and in an instant she was on my arm with one huge yellow foot on my fist, the other gripping my arm at the elbow. Instantly I stepped backward to the end of the leash, making it taut to the perch. In one gulp she had swallowed the meat, and now she was looking at me as if I had eaten it!

With slow, relentless force her talons tightened on my arm. I was frightened at her strength. Never before had I experienced her full power. The circulation on my arm was cut off, and my muscles ached as I tried desperately to maintain my arm in a horizontal position. I was struck with the irony of it all. For four days we had coaxed and begged this eagle to jump to our fist, and now that she had, I was praying that she'd get off! Each time my arm sagged below the horizontal, she would take a quick step up the arm toward my shoulder. It is the nature of any trained hawk to maintain the point highest on the arm. As long as the fist is in the proper position, the bird will remain there. But, in this case, my shoulder was becoming the highest point and slowly she was migrating there. All the time she glowered at me and uttered her angry twitterings. My arm now felt as if it belonged to someone else and I was just a horrified onlooker.

18

It was sagging lower now, and she was eyeing my shoulder, which I felt was just a bit too close to my neck. Suddenly she released her grip and jumped to the perch but rebounded at me almost instantly. Needless to say, I had already gotten out of reach of her leash and was beating a hasty retreat to the house.

Once again she had submitted to our demands, but in doing so had still retained her pride by demonstrating her ability to take control of a situation. Outside, on the perch, she stood proudly, her crop full.

At this time she was spending several hours a day outside, on the perch. She was fastened by the two leather jesses which, in turn, were fastened to a leather leash. While in training on the perch, she would try to fly off repeatedly, only to come to an abrupt stop in about six feet or so. We greatly underestimated the force of this eagle when purchasing a leash the first time. The first leash withstood this treatment only a few times before snapping. Fortunately we were outside with her when we heard the flapping of wings and the pop, as eagle and perch parted. She landed only a few feet away, however, apparently unaware that she was actually free. We retrieved her and installed a stronger leash. Two days later it too broke, and again we were lucky enough to retrieve her. Finally Dad purchased a leash "strong enough to hold a bull," and we sat back, secure that she was secure.

Then one afternoon we heard the pop of the leash and the swoosh of wings. But this time Lady didn't land; she began climbing out over the valley. Lady was on her way. I sounded the alarm and began running after her, trying to keep her in sight. She rapidly disappeared behind a row of eucalyptus trees. The situation was serious. She still had a section of leash attached to her jesses. She could never survive. A tangled leash would mean a lingering death. She

19

wasn't trained to come to us, so our only chance was to keep her in sight and pray she would land where we could reach her.

I came to a halt on the other side of the trees and looked frantically around. I was on a hill; the ground sloped off in all directions. Not a trace of Lady. How could she have disappeared so quickly? I walked toward a large oak tree, and suddenly I saw her, sitting precariously on a branch much too small for her. It is typical of young hawks to select landing spots that will not support them. She was teetering back and forth, and it was obvious she would soon fly. A few seconds after I spotted her she took off and began gliding toward me. At first I thought she was going to land on the ground by me, but I soon realized she was heading toward the valley behind me. Why, when she had a range of 360° to choose from, she chose a course that went right over me, I'll never know. As she got closer, for some reason she dipped low in what I thought was a farewell salute. She was on her way, I knew. Behind me the next range of hills was five miles away with a valley between—plenty of room for an eagle to get lost in. As she loomed closer, I realized for the first time how large a bird she was in the air. Her seven-foot wings and heavy body resembled a superfortress on a low-altitude bombing run. She was now only fifty feet away and moving about thirty miles per hour. Then I glimpsed the short piece of her leash dangling temptingly below her. I was struck with the thought that she was doomed and that somehow I had to stop her. She was approaching rapidly now, about ten feet overhead. I had a wild idea that maybe I could somehow grab that piece of leash. No time now to think about failure. With a wild leap I jumped high, hoping my timing was right. I had to reach the apogee of my leap at the exact moment she was closest. I felt the leather strap touch my palm and with all my strength I gripped it. My feet were jerked into the air as the momentum of the eagle was checked. We both were slammed down to the ground with tremendous force. As Dad came running up, he saw both boy and eagle flat on the ground, gasping for breath. The stunned look of surprise on my face was outdone only by the look on Lady's face. For hours afterward, she appeared to be in a state of shock.

From this point on, Lady's training progressed steadily, and so did our film. Although Lady accepted me as a trainer, I had to remain within certain bounds. It was obvious that with little encouragement she could turn against me. Dad was her first love; she respected him—indeed was devoted to him. So it was with prudence that we waited until last to film the first scene of the picture. In the film we wanted to depict how we captured a wild golden eagle that had left the nest. Of course, since we had gotten Lady from a nest, we would have to set up the capture scene. When we felt that we had all the footage shot on the entire film, we made plans to do the first scene.

This sequence would depict the constructing of a bow-net trap for capturing the eagle. This is a device that has been in use for centuries. When fully opened, the two halves of the bow form a circle of about six feet in diameter. Loose fishnetting is fastened to both halves of the circle; then one half is folded back like a convertible top. The net is carefully stacked, and the stationary half of the bow firmly staked down. A device to spring the other half is attached, and a line to trigger the trap is run to a nearby hiding place. When all was in readiness, we launched Lady.

She was a well-trained bird now, and we flew her often, retrieving her by calling her to a lure consisting of a piece of meat fastened to a weight. But this time as she flew we didn't call her, so she finally landed on a nearby cliff. Now we were ready. The cameras were double-checked. There

21

would be no second chance. I took my place in the blind as Dad put the decoy, a caged squirrel, in place.

From high on the cliff, Lady watched these proceedings with great interest. As she eyed the squirrel, she must have wondered what we were doing. Without hesitation she dropped off the cliff and began to fall like a bomb toward the trap. I tensed. I knew the camera was rolling and Dad was following her through the viewfinder. She hit the caged squirrel hard. I pulled the line and the bow whipped over her, carrying with it the loose fishnetting. As she began to flop about in the net, I rushed up with heavy gloves and proceeded to extract the screaming, thrashing eagle. There was one great difference between capturing this tamed eagle and a wild one. This eagle wasn't one bit afraid of me. Indeed, she was enraged!

I tried several times to catch her legs by the ankles to render her talons useless. Finally, with great effort, I grasped both ankles firmly and lifted her from the net. I then tied her ankles together, folded her wings, and placed her in a sack with just her head protruding. The entire sack was wrapped with twine so that she was unable to move. Then, while she lay on the ground as immobile as a chunk of firewood, I released the unharmed squirrel, gathered up the net and the eagle, and walked out of the scene. That was the end of the film and the beginning of a new chapter with Lady. For the next fifteen years she never willingly allowed me to touch her. She used every means at her disposal to let me know that I had committed the unpardonable sin.

The film was edited and submitted to Walt Disney Studios within a few months. Much to our delight the studio purchased the film, and it was presented on national television many times. This film was the first of many in which Lady appeared. She became one of the most photographed eagles in history.

ADOLESCENT YEARS

During Lady's early adolescent years, we learned much about the behavior and intelligence of eagles. My relationship with Lady was quite different now. No longer could I carry her on my fist or enter her cage. Many times I could only get within twenty feet of her cage before she would fly at the sides of the cage in an attempt to reach me. There was no doubt about her intentions. She learned quickly how to close her feet into a fist so they would fit through the three-inch webbing and then open them on the outside of the cage. All of this was done in a flash as the yellow feet reached a full twelve inches past the netting. Allowing for the stretching of the net wall, she could probably fling her talons almost two feet to the outside. When her momentum slowed, she would fall back to the floor of the cage. It was quite unnerving to be greeted that way. Strangely enough, while her attitude toward me was one of hatred and defiance, her attitude toward Dad was one of gentleness and devotion. What a contrast!

When visitors would come to see Lady, Dad would take great delight in demonstrating this behavior. I would remain in the house while they went outside to the cage. Lady would look them all over very closely. Everyone enjoyed her expressions as she took careful notice of a woman's hat or cocked her head to look directly into a camera. Perhaps, after stretching one huge leg, she would draw it up into her feathers and stand, oblivious of everyone, while she rested on the other. To everyone she looked as gentle as a chicken.

Then I would emerge from the house and begin walking the thirty yards to the cage. As soon as she saw me, her feathers compressed, her leg came down, and the feathers along the back of her head rose as she assumed the attitude of attack. When I was within twenty feet, she would fling herself toward me, crashing into the netting and grappling wildly with her feet. The startled visitors would gasp at so dramatic a change. Often she would exhibit "displacement activity" by taking out her rage on some inanimate object in the cage, such as the perch or a piece of wood on the floor. After slapping it around for a while she would usually repeat the attack. Everyone agreed that it would be suicide to go into that cage now. Then Dad would give the signal and I would return to the house, and he would go toward the cage. Lady's eyes had a wild, untamed look as she watched me leave, but then, as if by magic, they would soften—a visible, rapid change—as Dad approached. Little chirps of welcome would flutter up from her breast, and as he entered the cage, she would demonstrate her affection and gentleness by nibbling on his ear or tugging at his hat brim. The change was amazing and would almost bring tears to the eyes of the visitors.

We decided to test Lady to determine how acute her powers of observation were. We knew she had no trouble at all in recognizing me in a group of people, but we wanted to know how she did this. Eagles have little sense of smell, so we knew it must be sight or voice recognition, or both.

One day when we had some visitors, we decided to put the visual part of the test to work. I dressed up in my mother's bathrobe, put a shawl over my head, and joined the rest of the onlookers, feeling quite ridiculous, to say the least. As we stood there, I didn't say a word and just watched as Lady gave everyone the usual lookover. When she came to me, I shuffled with arms folded in front of me in a manner completely unlike my usual stance. She looked only briefly, then passed on to the next person. I felt somewhat elated that my disguise had worked and turned to smile at Dad. He said, "You'd better look again." She was staring very intently now, scrutinizing my costume and then again my face. Then slowly her feathers began to rise on the back of her neck while the rest of her feathers compressed. I barely moved and she lashed out at the webbing. Positive identification! The whole process had taken less than two minutes. She had identified me through facial features only, in spite of my being dressed as one of the opposite sex.

The audio part of the test was quite simple. While Dad observed her, several of the men stood out of sight and each, in turn, called the same words, "Hello, Lady!" She recognized her name and the greeting but did nothing to acknowledge it. My turn to call came. The instant she heard my voice, she turned to face the sound and flew to the perch nearest the voice. There was no doubt she recognized the voice. A few years later, when I was away at college for six or eight weeks at a time, she would always recognize my voice on my return, in spite of my long absence.

As long as Lady was confined in the cage or attached to the outside perch it was quite safe for me to walk the premises. However, when she was flying free, it was a different story. She claimed the entire hill on which we lived (about five acres) as her territory and was very diligent in keeping it clear of undesirable residents, namely, me. Fortunately, she never bestowed the same treatment upon visitors coming up the hill.

Usually the schedule was quite predictable, and there were certain times each day that I was confined to quarters. If I went away in the car for a while, I usually knew when it was safe to return. There were times, however, when for some strange reason Lady would be making an unscheduled flight. More than once these unscheduled flights just happened to coincide with my return from town. I strongly suspected Dad of planning this, but, when confronted, he would always have a very logical explanation. It was on one of these "coincidences" that I found myself halfway between the car and the house when I heard Dad yell, "Look out, she's at four o'clock!" I glanced back and saw her coming fast. I dived into the lemon grove and began a mad 20-yard dash between the trees, never slowing down until I circled back to the house. Fortunately the eagle, being an open-plains bird, is not apt at flying through trees. I became very good at it.

It was during one of these reckless dashes through the trees with Lady in hot pursuit that Dad got a brilliant idea. I listened with dismay as he outlined his plan for getting some "fabulous" shots of Lady. One of the problems of photographing an eagle in flight is controlling her direction and her movements. Of course there is the lure to call her with, but once that is done and the eagle has eaten, you don't dare fly her again that day. But the plan Dad outlined was one that would allow us to call Lady from any altitude, any angle, at any time, and as many times as necessary. His eyes glistened as he informed me that this sure-fire lure was—me! Instantly I began to protest but was soon buried under a dozen reasons why I should do this, along with glowing descriptions of the kinds of eagle shots we could get.

The first experiment was carefully planned. Lady's cage was about twenty feet long, and at each end there was a door. Lady's habit when flying was to land after ten or fifteen minutes in a large oak tree a hundred yards away. Time and again Dad tried to get a complete shot of her taking off from that tree and beginning a dive. But he would never know the exact moment she would take off; consequently, when she launched, he was always one second behind. The plan went this way:

Dad released Lady and unlocked both exit doors to her cage. When she had landed and settled in the tree, he set up the camera. I waited until he gave the signal, and then with great apprehension I exposed myself in full view to Lady some one hundred yards away. Instantly she launched toward me and began an ominous descent, punctuated frequently by determined beats of her wings. I turned and made a cowardly dash for Lady's cage. One glance behind me confirmed my suspicions that she was moving frightfully fast—faster than I expected. With a sudden surge of power, I burst through the cage door a scant ten feet ahead of her. According to plan, she followed me in. In the last instant before I reached the back door of the cage, the thought flashed through my mind that perhaps Dad had forgotten to unlock it. I'm sure it would have made no difference anyway because the speed I had attained would have carried me right through the wall! Fortunately the door was unlocked, and as I slammed it behind me, Dad closed the front door. We not only got the shot but retrieved Lady in the cage, all in one process. Dad beamed as he described the shot and the ease with which it had come off. I smiled weakly and said, "There's nothing to it."

From then on I became a "tool," as Dad persuaded me to

lure Lady in every conceivable situation, providing us with sudden dives, takeoffs, abrupt changes in flight patterns and spectacular studies in maneuverability. Always I was the hunted, she the hunter. The odds of continuing such activity unscathed were not too high. It is a well-known fact in nature that animals which are the prey seldom live to old age.

Lady could be fooled once or twice but seldom more. She was intelligent and calculating. More than once she followed me all the way to the house back door, crashing heavily to the wooden porch just as I scooted through the screen door. As I peered through the screen, she would clomp back and forth in front of the door, the clattering of her talons on the wooden porch sounding not unlike the rattling of sabers. She always knew exactly where the door closed against the jamb and would usually throw a few well-aimed blows at the crack with her husky feet. During these episodes Dad would get great delight in urging her on by saying, "Sic 'em, Lady." She would respond with arrogant display of posture and another volley of blows aimed at the door. On one occasion, at Dad's suggestion, I opened the door a crack to see if she really would try to come in. She reminded me of the stories of door-to-door salesmen getting their foot in the door. Once she had her leg in, she followed with her head and one huge wing shoulder. It was all I could do to force her back out, much to the enjoyment of Dad. I never tried that again.

It was always a bit humiliating for me to have to race to the house for cover every time she gave chase. Besides, it wasn't good photographically, because every time she pursued me, she took the same flight path and, consequently, all the shots were identical. We needed variety. Dad was of the opinion that she would never touch me. "She is only playing," he would tell me in reassuring tones. He used as an example the fact that she always chased the flock of white geese from the farm below, but always turned away just before making contact. With this bit of "proof" that Lady was being playful, I reluctantly agreed to try something different.

Dad cut a bushy limb from a sage and told me to use it as a shield and she wouldn't come near me. I took the bush and for the first time exposed myself to Lady without heading for the house when she spotted me. Instead, I headed out into the open field, clutching the bush, which seemed to get smaller and smaller the farther I got away from cover. She was about 150 feet high when she began her descent. Of course Dad was filming.

There is an unwritten code among photographers when filming unrehearsed action scenes: no matter what happens to the subject being filmed—*don't stop the camera!* I was well aware of this and knew that if I got into trouble I could expect no help from Dad until he ran out of film. Lady was fast approaching as I turned to face her with my shield. The bush had appeared quite substantial when Dad offered it to me, but now it looked very pitiful. Lady came straight in and then pulled up and hovered momentarily directly above me. Then, with talons extended, she dropped straight into the bush. I let go and fled. It took her a few seconds to untangle herself from the bush. By the time she was airborne again, I had reached a small clump of sage. Like a baseball player sliding in on first base, I slid beneath the sage. While I crouched beneath that bush, Lady swooped in and hovered about ten feet above me, waiting for me to make a move. She had me! I was experiencing the very same feeling a rabbit must have when an eagle has him cornered. I couldn't go anywhere, but the temptation to run was overwhelming. I froze motionless, hoping she wouldn't land and come in for me on foot. About that time

Dad came running up and, much to my relief, shooed Lady away.

She was making daily flights now, and they were frequently punctuated by passes at the flock of geese below us. We never flew her when there was any activity on the farm below, such as people, kids or dogs moving about. Always a phone call just before we flew her would let us know if it was clear below. However, sooner or later there was bound to be a slipup. It came one afternoon as she was gracefully working the updrafts along the brow of our hill. We didn't notice the station wagon coming up the driveway below us. We did notice, though, a sudden change in Lady's flight pattern. Her graceful sweep across the hill changed abruptly into a purposeful pattern. Her wings were carried a little low, and she began to quarter back and forth. Then, to our horror, we saw that the station wagon had unloaded two little dachshunds who were racing madly around the car and out into the field. Their owner was talking to the foreman, not noticing the eagle high above.

Lady began her ominous descent. We could see that she was picking as her target the dog farthest out in the field who was busy chasing butterflies and other such elusive prey. We tried yelling and whistling, but nothing could deter her flight. Her wings were half closed as she zeroed in on the unwary pup. We watched in horror; visions of blood, heartbroken children and lawsuits flashed through our minds. The pup saw Lady when she was about 75 feet away, and he lit out for the car as fast as his short legs could carry him, yelping for all he was worth. She closed the gap rapidly, and suddenly there was a cloud of dust as the pup rolled end-over-end in the dirt. From out of the cloud of dust we saw Lady pull up steeply just like a fighter plane pulling up after a strafing run. She returned to the top of the hill where Dad stood in shocked silence and landed on the perch looking very proud and, I am sure, expecting praise for her deed. Of course, I had retreated to the house by now.

The pup, in the meantime, had lost no time. He had landed right side up and continued without any loss of speed all the way to the car, where he made it up, inside, and onto the front seat all in one leap. The amazing thing was that he didn't have a mark on him and, even more amazing, the owner hadn't even seen the event occur!

After that incident we were more careful, but we could never solve the problem of the geese. They were always wandering somewhere in the field below Lady's cage. The flock almost seemed to expect Lady's daily dive on them, and they treated it as part of the routine, diving for cover when necessary and reappearing as soon as she turned away. Their whole attitude seemed to be one of concern for only the present, not the past. With their short memory the present became the past in about thirty seconds. Although we didn't encourage it, it was inevitable that she finally caught one of the slower ones as the flock made their mad dash for cover. It was a clean, quick job. She hit him with tremendous force in midair. He tumbled to the ground and never moved. She was proud—her first prey! The flock of geese hovered near the barn, peering up the hill where white feathers marked the spot of their fallen comrade. It was a full minute before they ventured forth again.

I should have realized that with the killing of that first goose went Dad's pet theory that Lady was only playing and didn't mean business. Although I wasn't aware of it, I, too, was a plaything of Lady's. I had invented (or was it Lady?) a new game that was quite thrilling for both of us. While she was out flying, I would dash to a power pole and stand behind it. I'd attract her attention by letting out a whoop, and she would immediately head for me. As she

31

made her approach, I would lean far to one side of the pole, urging her on by phrases such as "Come on, Lady, this time I'm going to let you get me." I would hold this position until she was only ten or fifteen feet away and had that look in her eye of "I've got him now." Then at the last instant I would jump to the opposite side of the pole and she would zip harmlessly past the other side, because at her speed she couldn't make a last minute correction. By the time she turned around, I'd be on the other side of the pole. She thoroughly enjoyed these episodes even though she missed. I probably enjoyed them more, because this way I didn't have to make a cowardly retreat. It was more of a sport. I equated it almost with bull fighting. The only difference was that, instead of a cape, I used a power pole.

One of the things that is supposed to separate man from the rest of the animal kingdom is his ability to reason, to assimilate the facts and take the proper action. The geese were an excellent example of creatures that couldn't reason. And unwittingly I, too, was falling into that category as far as my little game with Lady was concerned. The same thing that led the geese into a laxness was working on me also—repetition. We had played this game a number of times now, and every time it worked exactly the same. It was so easy!

She circled wide and began another approach toward my position behind the power pole. As usual, I leaned far to one side, giving her a good target. At the last minute I jumped to the other side and, to my horror, I saw that she had anticipated my move and was right in front of me! She had figured out why she was missing me and had applied the proper corrections. I had only time to duck my head. She hit the top of my head with her talons, the two rear ones cutting a V-slash in my scalp, ending at the apex. In an instant all the fun went out of the game as I realized maybe she did mean business. I slapped my hand to my head and there was real blood. I bolted for the house to check my wounds. It wasn't bad—didn't need any stitches—but I felt worthy of the Purple Heart.

Lady had a different look in her eye. She had finally made contact! It was as if we had been playing tag, and now I was it. The thought that bothers me most is that I fell into the same trap as the geese, with the same results, even though I am supposed to be a bit more intelligent. Lady was the only one that used any reasoning power! From then on I had a great respect for her weapons and her ability to use them.

A RELATIONSHIP
GROWS

Golden eagles are by nature monogamous, and when they mate, it is usually for life or until the mate dies. They are also homesteaders, staking out a territory of up to twenty-five miles square and remaining in the same area for life. A pair will actively defend their territory against intruding eagles and will always remain loyal to one another.

In Lady's situation, the hilltop where we lived was her territory. I was the intruder who must at all times be driven away, and as was to be expected, she showed the same devotion to Dad as she would have had for a mate.

When Lady was a little over a year old, I graduated from high school and left home to go to college. For Lady, I am sure, this was a sure sign that she had succeeded in driving away the intruder. Now, day by day, the relationship between Dad and Lady grew. There are rare people who have a gift of understanding animals, and I am sure my father is one of them. He was sensitive to her every mood, able to read the indicators of her inner feelings. These were subtle things unnoticed by ordinary people but as sure an indicator as the fuel gauge on a car. The compression of her feathers, the size of her pupils, her posture, the size of her eye shield, her blink rate, her sensitivity to sounds, and, of course, her voice, were all true indicators. As a result of his ability to read these "dials," Dad gained the complete trust of this great bird. Not only trust, but love, even adoration, if an eagle is capable of that, was her response.

Another factor was present that I am sure affected this relationship. Dad's vocation is aerial fish-spotting. For over twenty-five years he has flown his single-engine plane up and down the California coast searching for fish for the commercial fishing fleet. He is an old-timer in flying, with over thirty-five years in the air and most of it bush flying, the "seat-of-your-pants" kind that few pilots today ever know. Consequently, there is a kinship between him and Lady. Both are aviators, both earn their living from the air, and for both flying has to be second nature.

It comes as a surprise to most people that eagles, just like human pilots, must learn how to fly properly. An eagle must learn by trial and error, but for man too many errors can be very costly. Dad understood the air currents, the winds, and how they could affect an aircraft. These same winds would affect the eagle in exactly the same way. When Lady began flying, he helped her by showing her where the winds were best and could be used to her advantage. He was always thrilled when she learned a new lesson. Always there was a parallel experience in his early days of flying and learning crosswind landings, downwind drift in turns, stalling speed, and many other techniques.

Many times when she was learning to handle herself in the air she made the same mistakes new pilots do. The results, however, weren't disastrous, only humiliating to Lady. Although Dad always allowed plenty of room for her to make a turn into the wind as she approached the lure, she nevertheless made several highspeed tailwind landings before she learned that heading into the wind could slow her ground speed. These tailwind landings were hilarious as she tried desperately but to no avail to put on the brakes, always ending up in a jumble of feathers and looking rather sheepish.

For human pilots a cardinal mistake is to begin flying up a narrow canyon. If the canyon rises in elevation faster than the aircraft can ascend with full power, the pilot is doomed to crash. Lady learned that she too had limitations in steep climbs. More than once she was forced to land and continue on foot to the crest of the hill.

Through all her flight training Dad encouraged her, helped her to learn and praised her when she successfully completed a new lesson. The eagle seemed to sense that he was helping and responded with continuing trust.

But those days were over; now she was flying freely, using the winds and currents to her advantage as she gracefully soared the slopes on the ranch. There were limitations here too, however. Although most of the residents in the immediate area knew of Lady, there was always the possibility that a stranger might take a shot at the large bird as she flew. Most of her flights were brief and restricted to the area around our house for this reason. Dad longed to fly her somewhere else, some place where she could be really free, in her native habitat, a place where prey abounded and man was scarce. But there was always the thought that maybe when she found herself in her natural habitat she would reject this human companion and follow her ancestral callings. He would never know until he gave her the chance to decide. He had to do it.

Early one morning, Dad rolled the little red and white Luscombe observer out of the hangar, fueled it, and took to the air to search for just the right place to fly Lady. He headed east to the open desert country. He looked over many places, but none were just right. Finally, a hundred miles east, he found a huge valley, quite remote, covered with sage and carpeted with bright yellow flowers. From the air he could see hundreds of jackrabbit trails crisscrossing the desert floor. Only one seldom-traveled dirt road passed through the valley. He smiled to himself, "Yes, this is the place, and if she does decide to leave, it will be the perfect place for her to live." He swung the plane around and headed home.

By road it was over a hundred miles to the valley, much of it winding and hot. He knew that the ride by automobile would be difficult for the bird, and he debated on an alternate method of transporting her there. There was a skeptical look on my mother's and sister's faces when he announced that he and Lady were going to fly over to the desert together in his plane. "Well," he reasoned, "she's used to flying, and she certainly isn't afraid of heights." It did sound logical.

He began by removing the rear seat of the two-place plane and installing a plywood enclosure complete with small window and a comfortable perch. A few days before departure he introduced Lady to the perch. At first she was reluctant to enter the rear enclosure but, with encouragement from Dad, she became accustomed to the situation after a few days. The next step was to start the engine and let her sit there and get used to the noise. Occasionally she would throw a volley of blows with her feet at the front opening of her capsule. Dad would jokingly say that she really wanted to get up in the pilot's seat.

Now that she was used to the feel and sound of the plane, the time had come to take off. I am sure people still talk of that sight, the little plane taxiing along the runway with the head of a huge golden eagle peering out the back window; the plane roaring down the runway, into the air; and then, as the plane circled the field, the silhouette of the eagle clearly visible in the back seat.

Lady had been a bit nervous during takeoff, but now that the plane had straightened out and was heading east, she calmed down and began looking out the window just like any other tourist on a first flight. Dad turned around, grinned at Lady, and shouted a word of praise above the roar. Below them the coastal mountains slipped slowly past.

A few minutes more, and they were over the western fringes of the desert. Just for fun Dad put the plane in a slight bank and looked back to see how she took it. She rode it like a veteran, not leaning opposite as some people do. He rolled into a steeper turn, and she stayed right with it. Finally, he put it into a near vertical turn and looked back. She was calmly looking out the window. Even a shallow dive and pullup seemed not to bother her. The thought entered his mind that she probably could ride the plane through an entire loop, but fortunately, this idea was interrupted by the bright yellow desert floor far below them. He chopped the throttle and began the descent. Gently the little plane touched down in a field of golden flowers.

As he climbed out and turned to look at Lady, he thought she looked a bit odd. When he opened the door, he was greeted by an awful stench. Bits of her last meal were flung all over her cage. Lady was airsick! Dad had thought of all the problems of flying her except this. He put her on her perch in the shade of the wing and let her convalesce while he cleaned the plane.

Lady sat on the perch and gazed with wonder at her surroundings. The eagle is one of the few creatures in nature to enjoy the luxury of color vision, and the sight of the bright yellow flowers must have intrigued her indeed. She watched intently as a Say's phoebe hovered while catching an insect, then dashed away. Off in the distance a marsh hawk skimmed low over the sage seeking out its prey. Even the honeybees flitting from flower to flower below her didn't go unnoticed. As Dad approached her, she uttered little chirps of eagerness, obviously aware that something new and exciting was about to happen. With Lady on his fist, Dad walked out into the sage. She rode the fist easily, feathers compressed with excitement, eyes alert and searching. In response to Dad's words she chirped her eagerness and excitement. He knew that at any moment a rabbit might burst out of a bush, that he would launch her and she would be off. Whether she returned to him or took the option of gaining her freedom, he knew she would be doing what she wanted most.

Suddenly, not more than twenty feet in front of them, a jackrabbit burst out of the sage, going at full speed. Instantly Lady was off in hot pursuit. The jack ran in a straight line, clearing small bushes with graceful leaps, gaining a good lead on Lady who had to climb to an altitude of about fifty feet. Once she had gained a bit of height, she began to close the distance, but before she even got close, the rabbit disappeared. Bewildered, she landed on a low knoll, panting like a long-distance runner. Now came the test. Would she take off as Dad walked up? Hardly! She was glad to see him and greeted him with chirps that seemed to say, "What took you so long?" Relieved, he sat down beside her and noticed with interest that his brown boots were completely yellow, covered with millions of tiny pollen grains from the flowers. The yellow almost matched perfectly the yellow of Lady's feet.

While they rested, a tiny Costa's hummingbird appeared out of nowhere, its brilliant gorgets flashing like sapphires in the sun. It hovered momentarily in front of Lady, then shot straight up like a miniature rocket out of sight. Moments later it reappeared in a power dive directly at Lady, uttering all sorts of angry twitterings from the top of the dive clear to the pullout, a scant few inches above Lady's bewildered head. Again and again the attack was made, much to Lady's amusement as she nearly twisted her head off trying to keep the tiny creature in view. Finally, after delivering his entire repertoire of maneuvers, the smallest of birds zipped away.

Once again she mounted the fist, and Dad and she began to move through the sage. Several hundred yards ahead of them Dad saw a rabbit hop into a bush and crouch. He began walking toward the bush slowly. As they approached the bush, he began to talk in hushed tones to Lady. She sensed the presence of the rabbit, even though she hadn't seen it. As Dad whispered to her, she looked intently in front of them. She was quiet, as if she knew exactly what he was saying. When they were about ten feet away, out went the rabbit and off went Lady. She chased him several hundred yards before giving up and landing. Again she waited for Dad to come up and join her. He wasn't surprised that she couldn't catch the rabbits. They were much too fast for her unless she had the advantage of several hundred feet of altitude. The purpose of the trip wasn't to have her catch a rabbit, just to give her an outing and a chance to fly in a strange area.

Over the years many trips were made to this desert. Lady never tired of chasing rabbits and on one occasion very nearly made a kill. A rabbit she was pursuing took refuge in a shallow hole. Lady landed quickly at the hole and stomped about quite excitedly while waiting for Dad to arrive. As he approached, she looked up from peering into the hole long enough to welcome him with loud calls. It was obvious that she thought he would help her. She obligingly backed off while he reached into the hole and carefully extracted the squirming rabbit. Her excitement was high as he began walking back to the plane. She flew in tight circles around him, calling loudly, obviously expecting him to release the rabbit at any moment. Instead, he put the captive into a box because he intended to get some close shots of the animal later on.

This disappointed her momentarily, but soon she was again on the wing. An hour or so later, she again jumped a rabbit which she pursued until it ran into a large bush. From Dad's point of view, he was able to see the rabbit creep out the back side of the bush. It was obvious that Lady assumed the rabbit was still in the bush because she began tearing at it and peering into the dark interior.

This time, as Dad approached, Lady didn't welcome him at all. On the contrary, she took a defense position at the bush and dared him to come near. After all, he had taken her last catch from her. She wasn't going to let it happen again! As long as he was near, she stood ready to attack. Only after he left did she turn her attention back to the bush. That was one of the few times that Lady ever stood ready to attack Dad. Perhaps this type of provocation is one that could also lead a wild eagle to attack its mate. In any case, it proved once again that Lady's feelings changed dramatically when anyone tampered with her prey!

Lady was always busy looking at something. Many times she would stare intently up into the sky for several minutes. Then, after several minutes of searching the sky with binoculars, Dad would finally see a swallow or a very high flying hawk. The vision of the eagle is phenomenal. Often Lady picked out an object too small to see even with binoculars and followed it intently as it moved across the sky. There were times also when she would look intently at the ground several hundred feet in front of her, then fly the distance and examine a tiny insect crawling slowly along.

After several more flights, spaced by long intervals of just sitting, it was time to return. Lady didn't object too strongly to being put back into the plane. There would be many more trips to this valley. Perhaps through these trips Lady felt the kinship between her and Dad. She seemed to recognize that flying was her element and she actually saw things of interest on the ground below her as they flew. She must have realized, too, that Dad was in control of the huge wings that were bearing them aloft.

FILLING THE LARDER

Any pet that one may have in a household presents feeding problems—the problem is usually directly proportional to the size of the pet. This problem is compounded if the pet is a domesticated wild creature and is again compounded if it is a golden eagle or any other bird of prey which has very special dietary needs.

During the years we had hundreds of people come to see Lady. They varied from the professional to the field hand, from the informed to the uninformed. The most common question asked was "What do you feed her?" An amazing number of people are surprised that the eagle eats raw meat. Few people realize, however, that this diet of raw meat must contain a certain amount of fur or feathers if the bird is to remain healthy. As the bird consumes the meat, it swallows a substantial amount of fur or feathers along with bones of the animal. Both fur and feathers are indigestible and soon roll up in a ball in the bird's crop, cleaning the inside of the crop just like a bottle brush. One of the first actions of the bird in the morning is to regurgitate this ball of fur and feathers, or casting, as it is called. Often beneath favorite perches of owls or hawks one can find hundreds of these castings, each one a neat ball of fur containing an accurate index of the previous meals.

Many birds of prey are captured from nests each year by unauthorized and uninformed individuals. Many of these birds are fed a diet of hamburger or scraps from the table such as one would feed a dog. These birds meet a slow death in a few weeks, and the owners are unable to understand what went wrong. It is imperative that any bird of prey have a casting at least twice a week if it is to remain alive and healthy.

This requirement places birds of prey in an entirely different category from any other wild creature that is to be reared in captivity, and it was a major consideration when we first decided to take Lady home.

The basis of her diet had to be something we could depend upon from day to day. We began by buying chunks of horsemeat at the local pet store. We had a standing order each week until the price of horsemeat skyrocketed so that it was cheaper to purchase beef heart at the local supermarket. But this meat, of course, would only be good for three or four meals a week; the rest had to be some natural food so she could have a casting. And here the demand for fur or feathers could only be exceeded by Dad's ingenuity at procuring them.

The most obvious source of cheap natural food for Lady was road kills. That was the term Dad preferred to use to describe the wildlife that succumbed to speeding automobiles on the highways.

The advantages of road kills were many. It was a source that provided variety, for one thing. Lady dined on everything from small field mice to unfortunate deer. It was cheap. It was steady. Dad became a master of the trade. He could spot an object in the road a mile ahead. He could tell at a glance if it was a "good one" or if it had had a bit too much sun.

But there were disadvantages, too. He could never quite convince my mother of the necessity of this chore. It didn't take her long to realize that the Sunday drives he now willingly took her on were induced by a need for food for Lady. Since most kills occur at night, these drives were always taken in the morning hours, when the animal victims of the night before were still fresh. A "successful" drive might yield a jackrabbit, a couple of cottontails and a squirrel or two, all fresh kills. It was a family joke, albeit a rather gruesome one, that the vultures and ravens would have to get up early to beat Dad.

This kind of food-procuring had its bad moments, too. In fact, sometimes it was downright embarrassing. One time in particular he was going up a winding country road when, rounding a bend, he saw a "beautiful jackrabbit" with not a mark on him, right in the middle of the road. Quickly he pulled over and stopped. Hoping that no car would come by, he raced to the rabbit, picked it up, and was almost back to the car when a car rounded the bend just in time to see him fling it in the trunk. He gave the people in the car a weak smile as they passed and hoped he'd never see them again.

On at least one occasion of these highway reconnaissance runs there was evidence of another operator in the area. Dad spotted a fresh squirrel, but there was another car in front of him so he kept his distance. To his dismay, the other car stopped abruptly and the driver snatched up the prize with every bit as much precision as Dad had developed. To this day he wonders what kind of creature that other individual had in his backyard that would make him stoop to such tactics.

Another method of supplying natural food for Lady fell to me during the summer when I was home from school. Dad explained that there were millions of gophers in the alfalfa fields around the ranch, just waiting to be caught. So, with a string of fifteen traps, I set out. At first my luck was poor, but soon my average was up, and if it hadn't been for every cat in the county beating me to my traps, I'd have done very well. At any rate, during one summer I trapped and Lady consumed three hundred and twenty gophers.

When I left for school again, Dad was faced with the old problem. He didn't have much time any more to run the highways, so he tried to devise a method that could be used at home.

One day a pair of pigeons from a distant farm dropped in to say hello. As Dad watched them, he suddenly got an idea. He tossed some grain to them, and soon they were returning every day. Then one day he trapped them and put them in a special cage and announced he was in the pigeon-raising business. The rest of the family looked at each other. We knew what would happen. Soon the hen was setting and Dad anticipated the hatching of two eggs. In due time two squabs appeared. Of course he couldn't feed baby pigeons to Lady; he'd wait until they had their feathers. By the time they had their feathers, he had all of them named and couldn't bear to see them go. "Besides," he'd say, "I really need more breeders." One generation led to another, with very few pigeons ever becoming a meal for Lady. What did happen was that his small flock lured a neighboring flock home, and soon his feed bill for the pigeons far exceeded any good they were doing Lady.

Other types of fowl found their way to Lady's dinner

table. A friend of Dad's managed a duck-hunting club, and during duck season he collected all the mud hens and other non-game birds the hunters shot in desperation and brought them to Dad already frozen. This supply, used sparingly, could last several months.

There isn't a commander or a general in any war that doesn't hold a certain battle, a brilliant strategy, or other successful maneuver that he has carried out to be his "finest hour." In the war to supply Lady's constant need for proper food, the aforementioned episodes were battles. And, as in the case of every general, Dad also had his "finest hour." He unfolded his newest scheme to me one day when I returned home from college for a visit.

I noticed a slight smirk on his face as we walked out to Lady's cage to say hello. There didn't seem to be any difference in Lady. She certainly appeared healthy—obviously getting a good diet, I thought to myself. Then Dad edged over to a small feed shed adjacent to her cage and rattled the door latch. Instantly Lady's attention was diverted from me, and she flew over to the perch nearest the old feed shed, looking very eager.

"What have you got in there?" I queried. I knew he used to keep pigeon feed in there.

"Oh, nothing," he replied, obviously relishing my interest as well as Lady's. "I'll show you later."

All through dinner I wondered what was in the shed, but I never asked questions about the subject around Mother or Patsy, my sister. Finally, dinner over, I knew the moment was soon to arrive. As Mom and Patsy started the dishes, Dad acted a bit strangely—he asked Mom if he could dump the garbage! But from the expression on her face, it had apparently happened before. I followed him outside, but instead of going to the garbage dump, he detoured behind the sheds and ended up at the old feed shed.

With hushed voice that barely concealed his enthusiasm, he said, "Just look at this," and flung the door open.

Brown bodies! Everywhere. Hundreds of brown, furry bodies scurrying, running, falling over one another in an attempt to hide. The noise of several hundred tiny feet created an audible rumble as they fled. He looked at me and said triumphantly, "*Rats.*" As if it needed an explanation. With that he flung in the dish of garbage and said with a note of finality, "It'll all be gone by tomorrow."

It had started only a few weeks before when a pair of wood rats had taken over the feed shed. He noticed and threw them a few items now and then. Then one day he added a bale of alfalfa hay for nesting material, and he was on his way. Nature took its course, and the effect of compound interest now showed very vividly. One extra large rat with whiskers quivering peered out at the garbage pile. He was braver than the rest and obviously much older. "That's old Sy," Dad pointed out. "He's my breeder." I wondered how many of the others he had named too. Old Sy dashed out, grabbed a cantaloupe rind and pulled it back with him. Dad closed the door, and we returned to the house. "Remember," he cautioned, "not a word of this to your mother."

On my next trip home, he was anxious to take me out there again. This time when he opened the door there was the same mad dash for hiding, except there were a dozen or so that couldn't even find places to hide in the straw. He confided in me that they were "growing faster than Lady can eat 'em." He even had to start buying food for the rats! It was obvious he had to do something to keep the population down. One by one, he began to trap them alive until he had fifty or sixty left. Then he would cart them down the hill a few miles away and dump them all out in a field where red-tailed hawks hunted. Periodically he would have to "prune" them, as he called it.

The purpose behind this whole operation was to provide Lady with food. This it did with very satisfactory results. But the method which developed for feeding her these rats was quite interesting.

As has already been mentioned, Lady's cage and the rat shed were adjacent. They shared the same wall—in fact, there was even an old door between the two. When the rat population reached maturity, Dad began to tap them for a couple each day. Each mealtime Dad would enter the rat shed and reappear moments later with a meal for the eagle. Of course Lady watched this event day after day with extreme interest. Her curiosity about that shed grew day by day. As he entered the shed, Lady would fly over as close as possible to the netting and try to peer into the shed. When she couldn't see what he was doing, she would fly down to the partition wall and listen with cocked head to the wonderful sounds of feet pattering and squeaks of panic inside. She became very keen to the sounds from within. She began to spend several hours a day standing on the ground next to the wall, listening to the sounds and trying to peer through the cracks into the dark interior.

One day Dad got a brilliant idea to make the whole job easier. He could hardly wait for my next visit home to demonstrate this newest technique. He had cut a small hole between the two cages. On the rat side of the wall he had fastened a hinged door which remained closed all the time—all the time except mealtime. I watched as he walked toward Lady's cage. She was eager and chirped excitedly. As he approached the rat door, Lady jumped down and lumbered over to the hole in the wall. There she took up a position not unlike a batter poised waiting for the pitch. She tensed with eyes glued to the hole as Dad entered the rat shed. As usual, rats were scurrying everywhere as he raised the hinged door covering the small hole. It didn't take long for one rat to discover the new exit and take the fatal plunge through the hole. On the other side there was a clatter and crash, then a small squeak and it was over. Lady's reflexes were fantastic. Her weapons of course were her feet. But until the instant she saw the rat she was standing on her feet. She had to see the rat, jump up, extend her talons, aim, and descend on the rat all in an instant. Few rats ever even made it all the way out the hole before getting caught. She became so good at this that one time when two rats burst through the hole she nailed both of them.

Needless to say, this event was very exciting for Lady. For the rats, this hole meant one of two things. It could mean that things on the other side were better than where they were, since none of the outgoing members ever returned. However, we tended to believe that the rats were getting suspicious. Perhaps those last squeals were words of warning to the rest of the tribe. At any rate, it became more and more difficult to get them to go through the hole. It was almost as if they'd rather die than enter that hole. Lady would become very impatient and, instead of standing at the side, out of sight, she would bend over and peer directly into the hole as if to see what was holding things up. This, of course, had a tendency to discourage any rat who was thinking of going through the door.

We had been wanting to test Lady's intelligence in learning and problem-solving. The rat situation certainly was a strong stimulus, so we decided to take advantage of the situation. Since the rats wouldn't use the hole any more, Dad fixed the old door so it would open. The first time he tried this new method, he entered Lady's cage and encouraged her to go down to the hole. Then he opened the large door, and Lady wasted no time in charging into the shed. She thundered around once or twice before getting a rat. Then she returned to her perch to eat it.

Dad then fixed a spring to the door and a type of latch that could be pulled with a string. When the string was pulled, the door sprang open. He allowed the string to hang to the ground. The next day Lady got in position to go through the door. He knelt down beside her and carefully took the spring in his hand and pulled it. The door sprang open, but he shut it again before Lady could enter. She was bewildered and a bit annoyed at the interruption. Again he repeated the demonstration, making sure she saw him pull the string. Then he left the cage to watch. She stood there for a while looking at the crack in the door. Then she threw a few well-aimed blows with her talons at the door and returned to her perch. But the problem continued to bother her. She kept looking down at the door and at the string. Then Dad went into the rats' shed to stir the rats up a bit. The sound of rats in that room was too much for her. Down she plopped again and walked back and forth in front of the door, occasionally striking it. Then she began to look at the string swinging slowly before her. Carefully she leaned toward it and took it in her powerful bill. As she took a step backward, the door sprang open and in she bounced. While she consumed her prize, Dad closed the door and we returned to the house to discuss this new event. Less than fifteen minutes later, we heard her crashing around in the shed again. She had learned her lesson so well that we finally had to remove that latch because she was constantly in the rat shed.

These various methods of food-procuring provided not only food for Lady but interest and occasionally amusement for the entire family. At the time, however, it was serious business. There were many other attempts to solve this food problem; some worked briefly, others not at all. It is quite certain, however, that every method available was tried at one time or another during the sixteen years we had Lady.

When Kent and Lady were friends.

An everyday ritual—Ed launches Lady for her flight over the mountains.

Lady's large and airy cage was built right on the edge of a cliff.

Ed and Lady. Theirs was a deep and curious relationship.

When Lady was on the nest, Ed fed her by hand and kept the eggs warm while she flew.

Lady tending to her eggs. The large deadly talons become gentle.

Lady may be a bit befuddled by these odd looking eagles, but she was a proud mama.

Lady following the ducklings around to see if they want more dinner.

58

Ed introduces Lady to his granddaughter, Kimberley.

EAGLE SENSE

Our experience with Lady so far had convinced us that she was an intelligent and observant creature. There was no doubt that she possessed the ability to make calculating decisions when in pursuit of prey, or, as in some instances, in pursuit of me. We knew from past experience that she could recognize my voice as well as face after a long absence, indications of a good memory. Now we wanted to test her in a manner that would force her to combine observations and memory to solve a problem.

The first test is a standard one used to test observation and memory in animals. Three identical containers are used —in this case, black paint buckets. While Lady stood on an outside perch, Dad placed the three containers upside down on the ground below her. She looked at each briefly and continued to preen her feathers. Then Dad showed her a chunk of meat. This caught her interest immediately. While she watched, he placed the meat on the ground, then set the container over it, thus completely hiding it. Lady watched

61

this odd activity with great interest. She was then removed from sight of the cans for ten minutes. At the end of the time, she was placed back on the perch. No encouragement whatsoever was given her. She immediately began to look with interest at the cans. First, the first one was scrutinized closely, then the second, and finally the third. Then back she went to the first container, studying it with one eye and then the other. Her decision was made. Down she came and walked up to the end can, hesitated a moment as if trying to decide how to go about turning it over, then hit the base of it with one foot. With her beak she then neatly flipped over the can, exposing the food. Quickly she grabbed the meat and returned to her perch to consume it.

For the next six days this test was given each day, but each day the interval was lengthened ten minutes. Each time Lady promptly went to the correct can and easily flipped it over. It must be noted that olfactory senses of birds of prey are poorly developed, so that this could not be a factor in her detecting the meat.

After the six days her behavior began to change. She seemed to have lost interest in the test and would knock over the three containers at random until she found the meat. It was as if she was bored over the whole thing. She knew the meat was under one of the containers, and it was simply a matter of knocking them all over until she found it. Either we had reached the limits of her memory, or she was simply getting bored and mentally lazy. At any rate, the test was discontinued after the time had been extended to one hour.

A later instance occurred which strengthened our belief that her memory-capability exceeded the one hour with the containers. Dad was walking along a wooded trail with Lady on his gloved arm. As usual, she was very alert. Suddenly he felt her tense on his arm, and he knew she had spotted something. Looking up the trail a hundred yards, he saw a ground squirrel perched atop a rotten log. He knew Lady didn't have a chance of catching the squirrel, but she was eager, so he launched her. The squirrel watched her for a few seconds and then easily made it to a hole under the log. Lady landed on the log and stomped around it a few minutes, obviously irritated. Finally, after much coaxing, she hopped back up on the fist and, with many backward glances, was carried away.

It was several weeks later that Dad again walked with her along that same trail. He had forgotten the incident entirely, until he felt her tense on his arm again. She was looking intently at the log. There was no sign of the squirrel, but nevertheless she was excited. Once again he launched her. She landed on the log and walked all around it, peering beneath it and all the while uttering excited chirps. Her memory of that squirrel had lasted several weeks because it was a strong stimulus. It made an impression on her mind that was instantly recalled when she saw the log. Undoubtedly, if we had used a strong stimulus in the container test, the time could have been extended considerably.

Many times people who have been looking at the eagle will ask, "Does she do any tricks?" We never set out to teach her any "tricks" as such. The word "trick" conjures up such things as "rolling over," "jumping through flaming hoops," and so forth. However, if one defines a "trick" as teaching an animal to do something it would not normally do, then I would concede that Lady could do "tricks." Most, not all, of these tricks were variations on the same theme of obtaining a reward for an act. Unlike a dog, who can often be rewarded with praise, the eagle had to be rewarded with food.

We have observed from past experiences (the rat door) that Lady was quick to grasp a new method for gaining a reward. We decided to put her to the test of solving a problem in which she would have to observe the situation, adapt herself to it and solve the problem through her adaptations. As usual, the reward would be food.

As has been mentioned before, the sides of Lady's cage were covered with fishnetting clear to the ground. A three-foot piece of white string was attached to a chunk of meat. The meat was placed outside the cage, just out of Lady's reach. The string was laid in a straight line on the ground through the fishnetting and into the cage. Then Lady was called over to the side.

She could easily see the meat, so her first reaction was the normal reaction—to reach out and grab it. The problem was that, try as she might, she couldn't quite reach it. She spent a couple of minutes lunging at the netting. All the time this action was being recorded on film. After the first attempts failed, she underwent a period of what appeared to be contemplation. She stood there quietly looking around, at times seemingly ignoring the problem. Frequently, however, she would look intently at the meat, indicating that the problem had not been forgotten. What followed after that period of contemplation was incredible. The camera showed it very clearly. She leaned over, and with her beak picked up the end of the string and took a step backward. Of course the meat moved also. This movement of the meat triggered her natural impulse to strike. But the distance was still too great for her to reach. Once again she picked up the string, this time a bit closer, and took two steps backward. This time the meat was within reach and she got her reward. The amazing thing was that the total elapsed time was less than three minutes! She accomplished her goal by doing exactly the opposite to what is normal. In order to decrease the distance separating her from the food, she first had to increase the distance. In this experiment she had to observe that the string was attached to the meat. She then had to reason that by moving backward she could bring the meat closer. Note, however, that the success occurred only after she had exhausted all her natural methods of obtaining the reward.

We had substantial evidence that Lady recognized voices, and now we wanted to explore her word recognition. She learned early to recognize her name. There were indications that she also understood certain phrases, such as "go outside" and "sic 'em." We discovered quite by accident a little trick that used to delight her visitors. One day I went out to her cage with a soft drink in my hand. Just for fun I blew across the open mouth of the jar, making a low whistle. For some reason this low frequency sound caused Lady to open her mouth wide—gaping, it is called. Probably the frequency affected her ears, and she was trying to equalize the pressure. Whatever the reason, it worked every time. All that was necessary now was to associate a phrase with her mouth opening. After saying clearly, "Open your mouth, Lady," we would blow the whistle, and of course she would gape. We repeated this many times, and it was not long before she would gape at the voice signal alone.

Often when visitors were looking at her, Dad would tell them to notice her strong beak, and then casually tell Lady to open her mouth; this she would promptly do, giving everyone a view of her bright pink tongue and throat. Occasionally this came in handy when shooting film. If the script called for her to open her mouth, we simply gave the command.

Most people are surprised to learn that this warriorlike bird is very playful. Eagles have been observed in the wild playing with sticks and other objects on the ground. Young eagles, especially, will pounce on various objects while in a playful mood, thus developing skills that will later help them to catch prey. Courtship activities of adult birds often consist of playful diving and swooping on one another.

Lady, too, demonstrated a playful streak from the beginning. Often from the house we would see her pouncing on imaginary or real objects in the cage. Dad began early to cultivate this trait in her by joining in her games. He soon found that she loved anything that she could squeeze with her strong feet. He created the ideal toy for her simply by stuffing a paper sack with newspaper and twisting the neck until it was tight. Then he would toss it into her cage and she would spend hours bouncing around the cage with the sack clutched tightly in her feet. In due time she would tear it to shreds, thus bringing to an end her game for that day.

She looked forward to each time Dad brought her a new sack. He made a big production out of preparing her toy. She chirped excitedly as he wadded up newspapers and stuffed them in the bag. The rattling of the paper punctuated by Dad's smacking the sack between his hands and saying "sic 'em" really got her in the mood. He entered the cage with the sack behind his back. She poised, ready to catapult off the perch the instant he threw it. He said "sic 'em" and hurled the sack to the far end of the cage. She raced it to that end, where she pounced on it, giving it several death-dealing squeezes. Then she usually bounced around the cage with it in her feet. She so enjoyed his tossing the sack for her that the next step was to teach her to let him have it so he could throw it again. If she began to tear it up, he promptly left the cage. However, if she accidentally dropped the sack, he threw it again for her. She soon learned to drop the sack after catching it. But he wanted her to learn to bring it back. "If you can teach a dog to return a stick, you must be able to teach an eagle," he would say. He began by refusing to throw the bag if she left it anywhere but near him. At first she just accidentally dropped it near him.

After a few times, however, she learned and was soon catching and bringing the sack to him for another go-around.

The obvious next step was to expand this game outdoors where she was free to fly. Her eagerness was just as great, but now the method was altered. Instead of tossing the sack on the ground, we threw it into the air. Usually we put her on the perch and attached the leash. This was necessary because she was so excited that often she would launch before Dad could even walk out a few yards into the field. When he was in position, I would disconnect the leash and away she'd go; timing was critical. As she approached, he would have to throw the sack at the right instant so it would be at its proper apogee when she was in position. As the sack climbed to about twenty-five feet, she would climb to intercept it. It was a fantastic sight that we were able to record several times in slow motion. She never took her eyes off the sack. Steeper and steeper she would angle her flight until she was in a vertical position. If the timing was correct, she would arrive under the sack just as it started down. Usually at the last second she would turn almost inverted, extending her yellow feet skyward, and let the sack fall into them as deftly as an outfielder getting a high fly. The interesting thing, as could be seen in slow-motion film, was that no matter what position her body was in, her eyes were always on the sack. Occasionally she made wild one-footed catches. The instant the sack was in her grasp she would right herself and sail serenely off over the valley with the brown bag tucked neatly beneath her tail. The neighbors below us were used to the sight of the eagle with her sack. For the first few times this was done outdoors, she wouldn't bring the sack back. Instead, she'd soar over the valley and farms for a quarter-hour before coming in. Somewhere along the route she would eject her load and watch it plummet toward earth. The ranchers below would say, "There goes that eagle on her bombing run again."

In the interest of saving paper bags and keeping the countryside from being littered with paper bombs, Dad taught her to bring them back. This was done through a reward. While she was flying with the bag, he would whistle and place a piece of meat on the perch. If she dropped the bag en route, he would remove the meat when she landed. When she finally returned with the sack, she was rewarded generously. Soon the sack-catching was a part of her regular activities, and it came in very useful during the making of films years later.

An eagle in captivity requires certain attentions that at times become distasteful and traumatic for both man and bird. About four times a year it was necessary to "cope" the bill and talons of the big bird. The material of the bill and talons is a living material that grows just as fingernails do on humans. Periodically it becomes necessary for us to trim our nails. So it is with eagles. In the wild the bird grinds down its talons naturally as it lands on rocks; tearing at the bones of animals keeps the bill trimmed. Any bird which is restricted cannot possibly do these jobs for itself. If not trimmed down, the talons grow in a corkscrew pattern. I have seen zoo birds in some of the nation's best zoos in a pathetic situation, with talons so long that the poor creatures couldn't grasp a perch, nor could they walk on the ground without stepping on their own feet. The bills of some zoo birds have grown to such extremes that the mouth is perpetually open, eliminating the possibility of the bird's ever preening its feathers, and I wondered how the pitiful things fed themselves. Birds kept in this condition should be put out of their misery, and a fate worse than that should be dealt out to those responsible.

The job of trimming Lady's bill and talons was always

a two-man job. Lady's dislike for the process was only exceeded by my own. Dad found that he not only had to trick Lady into it—he also had to trick me! Usually he planned these trimmings secretly and didn't tell me until a few minutes before. Had he given me notice, I'm sure he would have been alone at the appointed time.

The tools used were simple: a file and wire cutters, the file for the bill, and both for the talons. Of course there was a leather jacket I wore in hopes it would ward off Lady's talons in case she got loose. The first time was probably the easiest. She didn't suspect a thing as Dad entered the cage. He walked up behind her and quickly grabbed each ankle and took her outside. I folded her thrashing wings and he laid her in my lap. Then somehow I had to get her ankles in my grasp so he could be free to work. This was the most difficult part of the job, since there was the chance she could get loose at that moment. She did everything in her power to break loose. Each time she shoved one big leg up, the talons came within inches of our faces. The first time we did it I was amazed at her strength. She had powerful legs and could almost twist them out of my grip. I held on tightly while Dad began the job.

Swiftly he filed her bill. The inside curve of the upper mandible had to be ground down, as well as the tips of both mandibles. She would groan and cry like a child as he worked. The wire cutters were used on the talons. First he would clip an appropriate amount off, usually a sixteenth to eighth of an inch. Then the file would have to be used to smooth the tips so they wouldn't split. Split talons can cause death in a bird of prey if the split travels up into the root of the talons. Throughout this whole procedure I had to maintain a firm grasp on the ankles lest she take me by surprise and lash out, catching one of us in the face. It was tense, tiring work. By the time we were through, her feet had gone to sleep, and when we dumped her back into the cage, she could hardly stand up. This didn't keep her from launching an attack, however. We only added to her fury by laughing at her awkward walk on numb feet. Wisely, we retreated to the house.

We weren't sure how this first bill coping would affect her. She was over a year old and well trained. We gave her a cooling-off period. Then, after changing our clothes, we returned to the cage. She was distraught, to be sure, but in a few hours it was as if nothing had happened. The ordeal was over, and we knew we were good for a few more months.

A few weeks later, Dad went out to the cage, and instead of being greeted as usual, he was attacked while he was yet ten feet away. She lunged against the netting in a serious attempt to inflict harm on him. No amount of soothing talk would do, and he didn't dare go into the cage. It was later in the day and several attacks later, that he remembered he was wearing the same clothes he had worn when we trimmed her bill a few weeks earlier. He changed his clothes and was greeted with the same old familiar chirps. From then on, those clothes could never be worn around her. She transferred her feelings against him to his clothes and to me. She refused to hold any feelings of hostility toward him, and a year or so later she transferred all her hostility to me. After the first four or five copings she forgave Dad almost immediately, but she never forgave me. Through the years I became implanted in her thinking as the cause of all this discomfort because, of course, it never occurred when I wasn't there. I was only an accomplice, but she judged me to be the cause and therefore guilty, and she spent her life trying to punish me!

Through the years she became very sensitive to goings-on about the time a new coping was due. She was so suspicious that it became a challenge to see if we could surprise her. One dead giveaway, of course, was my presence. She didn't have to see me, she recognized the car! The real clincher was if Dad laid any tools out on the grass. We had to be very careful. Toward the end of her stay with us it was getting ridiculous! In fact, our last try at bill coping was probably the hardest one since we began the operation almost sixteen years before.

At this last time, as on many previous occasions, Dad had to trick me first. By this time I lived in a nearby town with my own family. We often found ourselves up at "Grandpa and Grandma's" house on the weekend. On this occasion Dad put Mom up to making a big roast, and we were invited for dinner. As usual, nothing was said about coping Lady's bill that day. Little did I know that he had already laid elaborate plans. The tools were already in position to eliminate suspicion on both Lady's part and my own. When we arrived, I was hustled into the house because "dinner was on the table." Lady didn't know I was there. After the good meal he revealed his plans. I had no choice. Caught again! He instructed me to stay in the house as usual while he went out and caught Lady. Then I was to come running. We watched from the house as he tried to be nonchalant as he went out.

We will never know what tipped her off. When he got out there, she wouldn't let him get near her; in fact, he was a bit afraid to go into the cage with her. He returned to the house and tried several more times that day, but she was so suspicious that he had to abandon the whole idea. He finally announced failure, and, if eagles can laugh, I am sure Lady must have laughed with the rest of the family.

MOTHERHOOD

The very existence of nature depends upon its ability to reproduce itself. The life cycles of organisms include many different stages in some, fewer in others, but all stages within the cycles are aimed at the ultimate end of reproducing the species. This climax of the life cycle is called maturity. Maturity occurs at various ages, depending on the nature of the organism. For many microorganisms, "birth," maturity and reproduction may occur within a few minutes. Rodents and small mammals often will take only a few weeks from birth to the production of offspring. Larger mammals may take from one to several years to reproduce, even though physical growth has reached its climax earlier. In the case of man, usually eighteen to twenty years are required for physical maturity. However, man is the only creature that has the power of reproduction years before he is considered mature.

Birds usually require from one to four years to mature, depending on species. This maturity is usually a visible thing: the plumage of the male and sometimes of the female as well makes a distinct change. This change is usually toward a brighter or more striking pattern, a pattern which plays an important role in the courtship that precedes mating and reproduction. Golden eagles require one of the longest maturation periods in the bird world and, in contrast to most birds, their plumage gets a bit drabber at maturity.

Most people think of the golden eagle as being completely black. The young bird's first plumage, in reality, has a considerable amount of white. Certain marks distinguish the young golden eagle from other large black birds; namely a wide band of white at the base of the tail and white patches beneath and on top of each wing.

Each year, as Lady molted, her new tail and wing feathers had less and less white. We knew that she would soon reach maturity, but to us it only meant that she would lose her white markings and get golden-tipped head and neck feathers.

The approach of her fourth year brought no great visible change. But in her nearly mature body subtle changes began to occur. Glands long quiet now began to swell, and soon their juices would course through her body, causing many changes which would prepare her for this new stage of her life. These enzymes worked many miracles within her body.

The reproduction of birds differs from that of mammals in several ways. Mammals have two ovaries which, at appointed times, deposit eggs into the oviduct. This is called ovulation. The male sperm travels up the oviduct to fertilize the egg, after which it moves into the womb where it develops until birth. Birds, however, have only one ovary. Development begins when the male sperm travels up the oviduct to fertilize the egg. Then the fertilized egg moves down the oviduct where the shell is formed. Ovulation occurs when the egg is laid and incubation begins.

Since Lady had no mate, her eggs were not fertile. Nevertheless, her behavior changed and she began to prepare for the big event.

Things which before held no interest for her now were of the greatest interest. Sticks of all sizes were selected very carefully and carried to a corner of her cage. When Dad realized what she was doing, he carried in armloards of twigs and sticks and dumped them in a pile on the floor. We knew now that the nesting drive was upon her, but we thought that it would soon pass. After all, she had no mate to encourage her. She took great pains to select just the right twig from the pile on the floor and to insert it in just the right place in her nest. By now there was a large irregular jumble of sticks and twigs, not in the least resembling a nest. Each day she worked diligently, not at all losing interest as we thought she would. In between construction shifts, she sat out on her perch and sounded a new call. It had a mellow tone but was quite loud. It drifted out over the valley, carrying a message to a mate that would never appear.

Construction of her nest continued for several weeks at a steady pace before she slowed down. She then became very docile and at peace with the world. Even when I appeared, she paid no attention. This was extraordinary. I could go into the cage and almost touch her before she moved away from me. She never made any hostile movements toward me. Inside her, two eggs were approaching full size. The shells were still extremely thin, awaiting the penetration of viable semen from a mate who would never come. As the time of ovulation drew near, she began to add soft material to the center of her nest. Soon a small depression was formed, about the size of a soup bowl. Small feathers from the brood patch on her breast were added to the bowl to soften it. The cradle was ready.

It was at sundown that the first egg was laid. It was a large one, about four inches long, white but splattered with brown specks. She was obviously proud or her achievement but appeared not to be too concerned about it. Two days later another egg was added, this one pure white, and then Lady began to incubate in earnest.

She was a diligent mother. Hour after hour she sat on the nest, getting up only to rearrange the nest bowl or to roll the eggs over with her hooked bill. She could not know that the eggs did not need to be rolled over, that the eggs had never been fertilized. She refused all offerings of food for the first few days and then only accepted small bits that Dad fed her by hand as she incubated. She seemed to be determined to carry on with this activity, and it began to be a matter of concern to us.

Her eggs, of course, would never hatch. She was so faithful in her incubation that it grieved us to think of her great disappointment when at last she had to abandon the nest. An idea began to germinate in Dad's mind. When he first saw her eggs, he was struck with their resemblance in size to the domestic goose egg. Would she accept a replacement of a fertile goose egg for her own? It was worth a try.

The search was launched to find a fertile egg. Dad didn't have to search far, however, because among the flock of white geese on the farm below were several incubating geese. The problem was to find an egg that was in the same stage of incubation as Lady's. The incubation period for both geese and eagle eggs are about the same, thirty-three to thirty-eight days. An egg that was due to hatch about thirty days from the start of Lady's incubation was snatched from the nest of a loudly protesting goose. Dad hurried back up the hill carrying the precious prize.

As was by now her custom, Lady got off the nest as Dad entered the cage, and flew to a nearby perch where she stretched her stiff limbs and preened a few disturbed feathers. She always welcomed his visits and took advantage of the opportunity to get off the nest. She gave the impression that it was his turn to take care of things for a while now.

Usually he would fuss over the eggs a bit while she looked on proudly. This time as he looked at the eggs he carefully shielded them from her view and transferred the two infertile eggs to his jacket while placing the goose egg in the nest cup. Then, as usual, he walked out of the cage to where he could watch what was to follow.

In a few minutes Lady flew back to the edge of the nest and approached the egg cautiously. She always walked with her feet and talons as limp as if they were of rubber. If one of the talons accidentally touched the egg, it simply folded under harmlessly. This time she paused to look at the egg. Where, a few minutes ago there were two eggs, now there was one. If she noticed this difference, she didn't show it. She simply leaned over, rolled the single egg, and settled down on it as always.

As the days lengthened into weeks and the time for hatching drew near, we began to wonder what disastrous results would occur from our tampering with nature. Was the first breath of air destined to be the last for this innocent gosling? Would Lady's limp talons spring to life and snuff out this tiny creature the instant she saw it? What would be the effect upon Lady if nature required her to react this way? These and many other questions plagued us throughout the entire thirty-three days.

Throughout this period Lady sat serenely upon her nest, at peace with the world. Since she had no mate to relieve her in the incubation chore, it was a twenty-four hour job. Her day was broken up by several visits by Dad at regular intervals. In effect, he was taking the place of her mate, because only when he was present did she get off the nest for any period of time. We noticed also that her attitude toward me was different. If Dad was not present, I could approach to within a few inches of her on her nest. However, if he was present, she left the nest in a hurry to drive me away. It was several years before we fully understood this behavior.

During the incubation period, she was constantly improving on the nest by chopping up grass with her strong beak and placing it close to the egg. When she settled on the egg, she would tuck soft grass and feathers all around her breast to make an airtight seal. Once settled down like this, she looked so much like a mother hen brooding that visitors found it hard to believe this was the fierce queen of birds.

Early on the thirty-third day, Dad went out to the nest. This time Lady was standing and looking at the egg and chirping excitedly. As he approached, she greeted him with enthusiasm and again stared at the egg. It looked no different than before, but from within the shell a tiny voice could be heard calling to the outside world. The amazing thing was that Lady and the gosling had established communication even before the hatching! If the gosling was quiet for a minute, Lady would chirp a few times, and then the gosling would quickly answer. Conversely, if Lady was quiet for a while, the gosling would begin to peep until she answered him. In this way the gosling was reassured that a faithful parent was right there waiting for its arrival. If this gosling could have known who the parent was, it might not have been so anxious to enter the world!

After a few hours a small crack appeared in the shell, and for the first time Lady could see life moving inside the egg. She became very excited now and chirped loudly whenever the gosling slowed down his escape activities. This "talking" encouraged the gosling to keep working.

Finally Lady began to help the process by gently picking away loose pieces of shell. Little by little the gosling emerged, and when finally he lay in a tiny wet heap, exhausted from his activity, there was not a more proud mother on the face of the earth. All our fears disappeared with the sight of that fierce loyal mother standing proudly over that youngster.

To fully understand the problems that faced this unlikely combination of parent and offspring, one must understand the nature of each species. The goose belongs to a group of birds that are called precocial. This means that the young are active shortly after birth and can run or swim as well as adults, which is nature's defense for these creatures. Most precocial birds nest on the ground (although not all ground-nesting birds are precocial), and the ability to run is important if the young are to survive predators. The ability to ambulate shortly after birth serves another purpose also, for most of these birds are ground-feeders: they eat grasses, grains or insects. Thus, they learn to feed themselves as soon as they begin to walk. Examples of precocial birds are geese, ducks, chickens, pheasant, quail and killdeer. Although the young of these birds are able to feed and ambulate, they still need the protection and guidance of the parents for several weeks. Usually precocial birds have large families, which is another safety factor insuring that enough will survive to adulthood to propagate the species.

In contrast, there is another group of birds that is described as altricial; that is, they are helpless at birth and need the constant care of the parents for many weeks. Most birds are altricial; good examples are wrens (they are fed hundreds of times a day), robins, sparrows and, with one exception, the birds of prey. The exception is the burrowing owl. This small, long-legged owl lives underground in burrows and consequently is vulnerable to predators, such as

79

snakes and weasels. Nature has provided it with the ability to run rapidly soon after hatching, but it leaves the burrow nest only in emergency. This owl must be fed by the parents, however, unlike other precocial birds. It also may have large families (up to eleven), an indication of the high mortality rate in youngsters.

All other birds of prey are altricial. When an eaglet hatches, it is so weak and helpless that it can barely raise its head to pluck a bit of food from the mother's beak. Even after several weeks, the youngster can barely hobble around on weak and uncoordinated legs. At birth birds of prey have feet that are enormous compared to the rest of their bodies, and it takes them several weeks to literally "grow" to fit their feet. During this period the youngsters must be fed pieces of meat by the parents, because their feet lack the strength to hold the meat while they tear it with their bills.

With this understanding of the different natures of parent and offspring, the relationship of Lady and her "offspring" can be better appreciated. About the only thing the two birds had in common was that the gosling wanted to eat, and Lady wanted to feed it. There the similarity ended. Their natural instinct took over and produced some very interesting behavior.

As soon as Lady had recovered from the first thrill of motherhood, she became very busy with her new responsibilities. The first chore was to rid the nest of the now useless eggshell. This she did by picking it up piece by piece and dropping it over the nest onto the ground. She had to be very careful now with her talons; one misstep could kill her baby.

The next order of business was food. By this time the gosling had gained his strength and was sitting up, peeping for all he was worth. Lady was frantic. Her baby had to be fed. It was with great joy that she took a chunk of horsemeat Dad gave her. Instinct told her just how large a piece to tear off for her baby. With a piece of meat the size of a matchhead held gently in her bill, she leaned toward the gosling and chirped. To her consternation the gosling paid no attention, and, to make matters worse, the baby began to move about the nest, peeping loudly. Soon the gosling was racing over the pile of sticks with Lady following him around with outstretched bill, trying desperately to get him to take the food. After each of his excursions he returned to the nest cup and collapsed, exhausted. Then Lady would repeat the procedure again with the same results. As the gosling became stronger, he led her on a merry chase through the piles of sticks, frequently becoming entangled in the twigs. Dad was observing this whole procedure and could barely conceal his laughter at the comical antics; but to Lady it was serious business, so Dad approached the nest to see if somehow he could help. She was glad to have him come and help with this unruly child. Gently he would hold the loudly protesting gosling up to Lady's bill so he could see the meat, but no luck. One thing was certain, however—the gosling knew who Mama was, for as soon as Dad released him, he scurried over to Lady and dived beneath her breast. Still he was determined to act as nature told him to and refused all of Lady's offerings of food.

The effect on Lady was extreme frustration. It was a traumatic experience to have one's offspring refuse the basic need of life. It was obvious that Lady was becoming more and more discouraged, and as Dad moved closer to encourage the gosling to eat, she did something very unusual. She gently placed the rejected piece of meat upon, of all things, Dad's nose! To put it mildly, he was shocked. But he instantly realized that this was a desperate move on her part to fulfill the maternal drive within her. If he too rejected the food, it might have a deleterious effect on Lady. It is interesting to note that she didn't place the food at his mouth but on what most resembled a beak on his face! Casually he moved his hand up to his nose and removed the meat, keeping it concealed in his hand. As soon as she noticed the food was gone, she placed another bit there and the process was repeated. Eagerly she bent to her task. Here was one who appreciated her efforts, the baby be hanged! Eventually she "fed" Dad about a quarter-pound of meat and seemed satisfied she had done her part. The gosling had eaten nothing all day, and Dad had decided to feed it the next morning if Lady wasn't successful.

Toward evening both Lady and her adopted child began to think of bedtime. Lady began to cluck like a mother hen and the gosling hurried to her side and scooted beneath her breast. She fluffed her feathers and settled down, her baby uttering sleepy peeps from deep within her feathery breast. The first day of motherhood was over for Lady, and by her standards it was a miserable failure. But we were elated because she had not rejected this gosling and had shown every desire to mother it as if it were really her own.

The next morning Dad entered the cage and was greeted by the cutest sight one could imagine. A proud and fierce eagle was standing on the nest with a bright-eyed gosling peering out from behind the huge taloned foot of its mama. No other gosling in nature's history ever had a safer place to hide!

Lady appeared to be anxious to be about the business of motherhood again, so Dad gave her a piece of fresh horse-meat. The gosling was now almost twenty-four hours old and had eaten nothing since entering the world. Dad realized that he would have to step in and feed the little fellow soon if Lady wasn't successful.

Carefully she tore off a small piece of meat and held it

tightly between the halves of her bill. A clear liquid ran from her nares (nostrils) down her bill and saturated the meat. This was nature's way of making the meat more palatable for the young eaglet. The fluid is a sweet substance that not only adds taste but helps the youngster's digestion. As before, the gosling was scurrying about the nest picking at anything that looked palatable. Lady again followed him around offering the food. Each time she got him cornered she would extend her bill toward him. After a few unsuccessful tries by Lady, Dad was about to take over when he noticed that the gosling was looking up at Lady for the first time, instead of looking at the ground. Lady uttered a sound and extended her bill toward the gosling, and he responded as if his eyes had just now been opened. She held her bill still while the gosling picked the meat off the bill and swallowed it with relish. Immediately Lady tore off another piece, and this time the gosling was waiting to take it from her. Soon he was peeping excitedly while he waited for the next morsel. The crisis was over! The gosling had adapted to this foreign way of feeding and was now eating like an eagle. This was just the first of many adaptations both eagle and gosling were to undergo as this unique youngster grew.

Day by day the gosling grew, nourished by eagle's food. Dad became concerned over this diet for a gosling who, under normal circumstances, would be raised on grains and grasses. So he began to add to this diet a mixture of bread and milk. The mixture, in a plastic bowl, was set before the gosling, and it wasn't long before he was guzzling it down with great gusto. Lady soon recognized that the gosling liked this new kind of food. The next time Dad brought the bowl, Lady simply picked it up by one edge in her beak, carried it over and set it down in front of the gosling! As he ate, she even tasted a bit of it herself to see just what was so great about it. As far as she was concerned, he could have it! She didn't need a second taste. When the gosling finished eating and walked away from the empty bowl, Lady promptly picked up the bowl and followed him all over the nest, dropping it in front of him whenever he stopped, as if to say, "Here, have some more."

The next big crisis in this family was inevitable. It was just a matter of time until the gosling would find his way down off the nest and onto the ground. Of course by now Lady was used to his wandering around, and she simply stayed near him. When he made it down to the ground and into the outer part of the cage, she joined him by flying to the outer perch while he explored the floor. She was not in the least prepared for what was to follow.

Lady's cage was furnished with a large bathing pool about four by three feet across and ten inches deep. Eagles frequently bathe thoroughly and, in fact, will often get sick if not allowed to bathe. *Grown* eagles, that is. No eaglet could ever survive, much less enjoy, a bath in that pool. Consequently, when Lady saw her youngster making a beeline toward the pool, she hastened to intercept him. But nothing could keep that gosling from entering the water, not even a very concerned mother. He quickly dodged between her legs and, with an excited peep, splashed into the water.

This was heavenly! Nothing could have suited him better. Why, it was almost as if he was born to swim! As he paddled around and around, he was not the least bit aware of the great anxiety he was causing his mother. Lady stood on the edge of the pool trying every way she knew to coax him from that water. Each time he came near her, she would lean far out over the water and try desperately to "talk" him back. But no luck. Finally, after several minutes of fruitless efforts, she did the only thing available to her. She joined him, much to the gosling's delight. As she waded into the water, he raced about, diving between her legs and popping up on first one side and then the other. Through it all, she tried to maintain her eagle dignity and seemed determined not to be ruffled by the latest antic of this juvenile delinquent.

As the gosling grew, it was very clear that he thought Lady was truly his mother. This came as no surprise to us, however, because many fowl, especially ducks and geese, will accept the first thing they see as their parents. This is called "imprinting" and just about any substitute for a mother will work. Humans, dogs, cats, chickens and even mechanical devices rigged up by experimenters have been imprinted upon young fowl. And now an eagle, its arch enemy!

Less experimentation has been done at the opposite end of the scale, namely, imprinting upon the parent. It is known that hens and ducks will raise each other's offspring if the eggs are switched, and nature has a classic example in the case of the cowbird which lays its eggs in the nest of another species and leaves the entire raising to the foster parent. The foster parent seems not to notice the difference in size (often the foster parent is much smaller than the cowbird) and dutifully cares for it.

In the case of our eagle, it was obvious that both parent and offspring had been imprinted upon each other. The differences in the nature of the two birds were overcome by this common bond of imprintation. There were times, however, when Lady appeared to actually notice that there was a difference between her baby and herself. On one occasion while she was lying down in the nest with her baby snuggled up to her, she began to scrutinize the gosling's feet. Then she ever so gently leaned down and nibbled the web between the toes of the gosling as if to say, "This youngster is going to have one hard time killing a jackrabbit with feet like this!"

Anything she may have noticed different about this baby didn't diminish her devotion to, and fierce protection of, him. From the instant he hatched, she had become a protective mother. Her hostility toward me increased dramatically, and for the first time she was aggressive toward total strangers. As long as her baby was near her, she would tolerate people, but if she thought anyone was a threat to him, woe unto that person! For this reason, we had to caution visitors to stay back from the sides of the cage.

The only human allowed near her baby was, of course, Dad. He was completely welcome in her eyrie, and she wholly trusted her youngster to him. As the gosling grew larger, bedtime became quite a problem. It was his habit to snuggle beneath Lady's breast for the night. This was no problem when he was tiny, but by now he was the size of a small chicken, and he still insisted on getting beneath Lady. As she lay on the nest, the gosling would begin to force his way beneath her. With a painful expression Lady would try to accommodate him by rising up a bit and giving him room. He took advantage of this, and as Lady settled down again she looked like a boat that had been left high and dry at low tide. One side of her was on the nest, the other side half in the air with the gosling crammed beneath. To make matters worse, the gosling would change positions several times before going to sleep. Each upheaval would nearly throw Lady off the nest. Finally this ridiculous pair would drift off to a fretful slumber.

By early summer the gosling was almost full size and had most of his white feathers. Lady was flying again and the goose had the run of the place. When Lady took off on her first flight, we had certain fears. The goose was now all white and he looked exactly like the dozen or so in the flock on the farm below. On previous occasions, Lady had made a meal of a couple of those white geese, so they were not unfamiliar to her. We worried that, once in the air, she would see the flock below, see the white one who now stood clearly in the open honking at her, completely unafraid, and instantly recognize that that fool goose on the hill was good to eat.

As she circled out over the valley, she instinctively dipped toward the flock, just to see them run for cover more than anything else. On the hill her "baby" stood spraddle-legged, calling out to her. She completed her circle and began to head toward the hill, dropping a little to gain speed. Still the gosling stood there in the bliss of ignorance as the huge eagle bore down on him. We thought, "This is it. She has finally realized what kind of a creature she was tricked into raising." Swiftly she closed the remaining twenty feet, and suddenly the gosling's honks of welcome turned to squawks of terror as instinct took over from imprinting at the last moment to tell him that he was in danger. He tried awkwardly to run, but slipped on the grass and fell flat on his rear just as Lady swooped over his head and landed beside him. Fortunately for the goose, Lady's instinct didn't take over at the last instant. She was merely trying to coax him into the air, but to no avail. Many, many times she performed this maneuver, hoping to coax him into the air or else to scare him into flying. The only reaction she ever got was an awkward, erratic run, accompanied by loud squawks and flapping of wings. He never did fly.

By midsummer the goose was full grown. Lady still provided his food, but now he would tear into meat as ferociously as an eagle, and he could do remarkably well with the tools he was equipped with. Though he was fed primarily on vegetation, he never turned down the chance for flesh food. A visitor who might happen to see the goose tearing into a jackrabbit, or as on one occasion, trying to swallow a snake, might be hard to convince that we weren't experimenting with a secret drug that would change all mice into lions.

From our observations, we were certain that this goose didn't measure up in intelligence to the eagle. We decided to try one experiment. Dad filled a bowl with the goose's favorite mixture of bread and milk and placed it in front of him. Instantly he began slurping and enjoying the treat. Then Dad took the same black container that we had used to test Lady some months before and covered the dish. It was incredible! With bread and milk still running out its mouth, the goose looked at the spot where moments before there had been food and simply turned away, as if it all had been his imagination! Removal of the cover triggered a rush for the now visible food; covering the food stopped him just as if there had been nothing there. We tested him no further. Apparently none of Lady's intelligence had rubbed off on this foster child.

From the beginning of the nesting activity, we filmed in both motion pictures and stills the entire story of Lady's motherhood. We obtained some of the most unusual footage ever filmed by anyone. I submitted a series of stills along with a story to *Look* Magazine. They published the story which told briefly of this adoption. Several pictures were used, including one which showed very clearly the gosling accepting a piece of food from Lady's beak. A few weeks after publication of this story, I received a letter from a research biologist at Oxford University in England. In the letter this gentleman explained that he had just completed a thesis on the domestic goose. He went on to say that he had performed exhaustive research with the goose to see if it could be induced to take food from a donor. His findings were that the domestic goose would not accept food from any donor. He therefore requested me to supply him with a statement that the picture in *Look* Magazine was a fake, and that this goose did not accept food from the eagle.

I promptly answered the Englishman and informed him that the picture was not faked, and that we had many more stills, as well as thousands of feet of movie film, of the eagle feeding the goose. I never heard from him again, and I suppose that poor Englishman is still working with the domestic goose!

A NEW HOME

During the first four years of Lady's life, there were a number of incidents that made us subtly aware that our house on the hill was not exactly the ideal place to raise an eagle and let her fly free whenever she wished. The incident of the two dogs being chased by Lady was followed eventually by a similar incident with the neighbor's cat.

As Lady was flying one day, she spotted a large black cat in the field below and began her descent. The cat instantly spotted her and lit out for the house at full speed. It was obvious that the cat would win the race to the house until, for some unexplained reason, the feline made a course correction that took it toward the orchard. It was then, to our horror, that we saw why. The cat had spotted its mistress, the lady-owner of the farm below and our landlady, and was making for her. Lady made a neat correction to this new course, added a few powerful beats to her wings, and rapidly closed the gap. The poor woman was not aware of anything until suddenly the cat screeched to a halt at her feet and began to gyrate back and forth nearly knocking her down. Before she could gather her wits about her at the cat's strange behavior, the eagle arrived with a swoosh above her and began hovering, waiting for the cat to make a break. Obviously the cat was not going to leave this place of refuge. With one hand trying to hold the panicky cat off, and with the other trying to shoo away the eagle, the poor woman had her hands full. It was not until Dad raced down the hill that Lady finally left the frightened pair and returned to her perch. With much embarrassment, Dad apologized and returned home, certain that an eviction notice was forthcoming.

The eviction notice never came, but we did detect a bit of coolness on the part of our landlady as well as of some of the neighbors. There were several cats that had mysteriously disappeared from the area, and although no one had seen Lady catch them, suspicions were very strong. Dad began to look for another house.

In the past, all the homes we had lived in were, like this current one, rented. Dad had an uncanny affinity for finding houses that were remote. I can vividly recall rides on weekends when Dad would spot a lonely house, far off the road, that appeared vacant. While Mom and my sister remained in the car, Dad and I would hike up to the house. He would peer into all the windows and then, at my insistence, lift me up so I could see the dusty interior. Then somehow he would find the owner, make a deal, and that would be our home for a while, until for some reason we would have to move. That was long before Lady's time, but even then we always had other animals or hawks.

Through all these years my dear mother hardly said a word about never owning our own home, but always gladly pitched in to clear out an old house and make it home. And now it was time again. But this time there was a difference.

I was off at college and would soon be married. My sister, Patsy, would soon be on her own, and for the first time in Mom and Dad's life they could afford their own home. They both agreed that the time had come to buy their own place.

After all these years of living in someone else's home, usually an old one away from people, Mom had a few ideas of her own. While Dad searched the hills and remote canyons, she looked in the small town near us at the neat homes with all their modern facilities, nice yards and neighbors to visit with. She even went as far as to make an appointment with a realtor to see a particular modern ranch-style house that pleased her. Dutifully Dad went along to see the place and to listen to its virtues as extolled by the realtor and Mom. It was a nice place, Dad agreed, and the price was right. On the way home he reminded her of what she had so obviously forgotten. "What about Lady?" he asked.

It was true. This place would be no place to keep Lady. Once again Mom had to play, as she said, "second fiddle to an eagle." It was a family joke that when Dad returned from an absence of a few days, he would ask, "How is Lady?" and then as an afterthought, "How are you and the kids?"

The search continued. A realtor was contacted who said he could find just what they wanted. Their needs weren't difficult; in fact, the house mattered little; the location *did* count. Countless times he took them out to look at a "jewel." Probably he never again will have such difficult prospective buyers. The first thing Dad would do was look over the property. Often he wouldn't even get out of the car. A line of powerlines across the view made it difficult for Lady to fly. "Don't you even want to look at the house?" the realtor queried. Dad just shook his head.

He rejected other houses because the sun was at the

wrong angle for shooting movies, or because the prevailing wind was wrong for Lady to fly easily. Perhaps the view from the house *was* fine, but Lady would have to circle over a group of houses. On yet another one: "Yes, the living room is beautiful, but there is a highway down over the hill."

"But you can't even see it!" wailed the realtor.

"But motorists can see Lady as she flies," answered Dad, as he walked toward the car.

"Lady? Who's Lady?" questioned the realtor.

"An eagle," Mom would say. And then, confidentially to the realtor, "What we are looking for is a home for an eagle. It has to be remote, high, with the wind going uphill—no powerlines, and the sun must shine toward the wind. There must be no houses or roads visible in the distance, and as Lady flies, she must not have to pass over any roads or houses. That's what Lady needs, and I would like two bathrooms."

The weeks went on with no success. Realtor after realtor gave up in exasperation. Finally one salesman, in desperation, said he did have one listing, but the road going to the house was terrible, and the place was small.

"Let's look at it," said Dad.

The clue that the place was promising was that the road was "terrible." True to the realtor's description, the road was bad, full of chuck holes and obviously not well-traveled. It wound past a few small, unkempt homes and up an oak-covered canyon.

"The place is clear at the end of the road," the realtor said, as he negotiated a particularly rough stretch.

Dad looked at Mom. That was a good sign. They crested a knoll, and below them was the house. They were at the top of the coastal range of mountains behind Santa Barbara.

Located on three and one-half acres, the small house stood well back from the slope. The canyons and hills

94

around the house were covered with oaks. Dad walked out on the point. The wind was blowing briskly toward him, up the hill. The sun was warm at his back, and the distant range of mountains with its shadowed canyons was beautiful. The oak-covered slope dropped off rapidly to the Santa Ynez Valley. As far as the eye could see, not a house or road was visible. On a ridge a quarter-mile away, a red-tailed hawk soared easily on updrafts. From down in the canyon, the call of the Gambel's quail drifted up. Dad took a deep breath of the sage-tinged air and turned toward the house. In his mind it was all settled. This was the place. But he would go through the ritual of inspecting the house.

Actually, the house was much nicer than they expected. It was small, but it was well built of old adobe brick—some were two hundred years old, salvaged from an ancient wall at the Santa Barbara Mission. The kitchen was modern and the living room was charming, with a huge fireplace and old hand-hewn log beams for ceiling braces. Even Mom was impressed. They could expand it to include another bath, Dad promised. The deal was made and the realtor, no doubt, is the only one to have ever sold a house because of an eagle.

Preparations had to be made before they could move. True to his promise, Dad expanded the house to include not only another bath, but another bedroom and a large living room with a huge window so they could see the view. Many considerations were taken into account before deciding where Lady should have her cage. Finally it was decided to put it right out on the point, even though that did spoil the view from the house a bit. There was a natural rock formation on the point that Dad constructed the cage around. It was a larger cage than the old one, and it contained a natural rock ledge for the nest. The huge doors opened wide enough so Lady could fly directly to and from her nest. The hill dropped off abruptly from her cage, providing her with a natural launching point for flights out over the canyon.

Eventually all preparations were made, and the family possessions were hauled up the bumpy road and placed in their respective rooms. On the last day Lady was put into her traveling cage in the back of the station wagon and driven the fifty miles to the new home. Dad carried her over to the new cage and put her on the perch. She looked curiously at everything and studied intently the perches and the rock ledge which Dad had already piled with a few sticks. After exploring her new quarters, she began to look out over the valleys. Her powerful eyes searched the distant range of mountains; she spotted a red-tail hawk high above the valley, and the movements of a brown towhee in the bushes nearby. It was obvious that she approved.

After a few days in the cage to get accustomed to the place, she was put outside on the perch with the leash attached. In just a few minutes, a tiny hummingbird discovered her and began his dive-bombing attack. Soon a scrub jay spotted Lady and set up a scolding designed to warn everyone of this intruder upon their area. A crow also took up the scolding from the safety of a tree top. From everywhere, all nature seemed to be turning out to give this newcomer a not-so-welcoming welcome. Through it all, Lady remained unruffled. She was thoroughly enjoying all the attention and couldn't care less what they were saying to her. From the comfort of the large living room, Dad and Mom looked out over the scene. This was indeed a place for an eagle and, as Mom had to agree, the house was very nice, too.

Spring was approaching. The hills were covered with green, the oaks were verdant with new growth. Pairs of red-tailed hawks circled daily over the valley, diving and swooping in their courtship displays. A small house wren braved the presence of Lady to investigate a potential nesting site under the eave of her cage roof. A western fence lizard sunned itself unconcernedly on a rock just outside the cage. And within Lady's body the nesting instinct was again stirring. Spring could be felt.

We were concerned that moving Lady at this late date in the year would affect her nesting behavior. Through all the house-hunting, this had been a pressing motivation. The move was made in late January. By the middle of February, Lady was selecting choice sticks and constructing her nest on the rock ledge. By the first of March she had completed her nest and had become very docile. On March 7 she laid her first egg; the other followed three days later. This year it was a white one first and then a speckled one. There has been much dispute as to which one is laid first by wild eagles. It was theorized that the speckled one was laid first, and then, since the pigment was used up, the white one. But we found that, on the average, the white was laid first in Lady's case. Usually, but not always, a speckled egg followed within a day or two. All her eggs, about twenty in all, are now being studied by the Santa Barbara Museum of Natural History.

Once this second egg appeared, she began to set. For want of a better substitute, Dad again replaced her infertile egg with a goose egg. After the prescribed incubation period, she was again the proud mother of an active gosling. She took it all in her stride this time, apparently satisfied that this was all part of motherhood.

Dad was eager to let Lady fly in this new location, so as soon as the gosling was up and about, he opened the cage door. With the strong motivation to return to her nest Lady was in no danger of leaving the area.

Gracefully she dropped off the ledge and plummeted downward for a moment before opening her wings fully.

When she had plenty of speed, she opened her wings and swooped up into the wind. As the wind moved up the slope, it carried her aloft, and she played the wind like a great musician playing a fine instrument. Her huge wings gathered wild energy in the winds and transferred it into forces that could propel her in any direction she wished. Dad watched in awe as she worked her way along the slope, hardly ever flapping, but always twisting, angling, and maneuvering her wing and tail surfaces to control her movements. He realized that here was the opportunity to record on film the full grace and beauty of the golden eagle in flight as few men have ever seen it. Although she was hundreds of feet above the ground, she was at eye level to him and only a hundred yards away. Far below her, the Santa Ynez Valley spread its green oak-studded fields, and in the distance Figueroa Mountain loomed through the haze.

As she soared, her head swiveled back and forth as she studied the ground below, but frequently she glanced back at the cage to check on her baby, who was happily rummaging about the nest. Of course Dad was standing by the nest, should the gosling need any help. Apparently assured that all was well, she suddenly shot up as if she were riding an invisible elevator. The change in her flight surfaces was so slight that it was impossible to detect it. Now, a thousand feet above her eyrie, she was in full command of the elements. As Dad stood with head back, watching, he saw high above her a tiny speck. He recognized it as a red-tailed hawk, and one who probably had a nest in the area. Lady was about to have her first encounter with the neighbors. The silhouette of the hawk now changed to a shape resembling a missile, and indeed it was a missile. The hawk hurled straight downward toward Lady, letting out screams of defiance as it closed the gap. At first it didn't appear that Lady was even aware of the hawk. Her flight pattern hardly changed. But as the hawk reached a critical point, Lady executed a snap roll, and extended her talons upward while in inverted flight. The hawk pulled sharply up just out of reach of those talons and shot back up into the sky. As Lady regained flying position, the little hawk made several more attacks before retreating to its eyrie.

Once the hawk was gone, Lady pulled her wings in until she had a delta-wing configuration with very little wing surface, and began to plummet toward her eyrie. As she neared the eyrie, Dad could see the feathers on her back being sucked upward as the air flowed over the airfoil of her back, creating a low pressure area exactly as do the wings of an aircraft. The wind whistling through her feathers was an audible whisper, getting louder until it became a roar as she opened her wings at the last instant to break her speed. She landed on a stump outside for a moment, chirped a greeting to Dad and looked skyward. She uttered a few loud calls at the unseen redtail and entered the cage to go to her youngster.

As Dad closed the door to her cage, he felt deeply moved. This was an experience that perhaps no man has ever before taken part in. It is true that men before have observed wild nesting eagles, but only as outsiders looking on from a concealed viewpoint. But this was entirely different. Few men before have ever stood in full view of a nesting eagle and watched the wild free flight of that eagle as she rode the winds and defended her territory against other birds of prey. Few men have ever experienced the exhilarating plunge toward earth of an eagle, heard the wind screaming through the wings as the huge bird braked to a stop a few feet before him. Few have ever witnessed the change that occurs when a screaming, defiant eagle turns into a gentle mother hen. But no man has ever been a part of this experience. It moved Dad because this great bird fully accepted him into her life and allowed him to fill the gap left by her natural mate.

This new home, although about as ideal as one could wish, did have some minor problems. There were neighbors, although most were out of sight, hidden beneath the dense oaks. Where one finds man, one usually finds man's best friend, the dog. Since the house had been unoccupied for several years, the local dogs had become accustomed to snooping around the property at will. (Not that it made much difference to them if the house was occupied.) Of course now that the house was occupied, they were even more curious about it. It was only a matter of time until they became "educated" as to the occupant of the "house" out on the point.

One day a Dalmatian worked his way along a path to the house. He walked with an air of complete control of things. These were his paths, this was his property, the new occupants of the house were the intruders. His nose told him that there was no dog in this new house to challenge him, so he was completely unafraid. First, he worked the trash barrel over to see if there were any scraps he wanted, then he sniffed the tires of the car, and finally, he became so bold as to go up to the back door and gobble up a dish of food left out for my sister's cat. Then, casually, he worked around to the front of the house, sniffing at every bush and rock. Occasionally he found bits of meat on the ground, scraps dropped probably when Dad walked out to Lady's cage to feed her. With his nose glued to the ground, he was unwittingly being led directly toward the cage. Perhaps he had been in the area around the cage before Lady had arrived, but it was obvious that he was completely unaware of the piercing eyes that now watched him get closer.

Little by little, his nose led him on until he found an especially nice tidbit at the base of Lady's outside perch, a scant ten feet from her cage. She watched carefully. He was not a small dog, but as far as Lady was concerned, nothing was too large when she had a youngster to protect. He finished the tidbit, ambled over to the edge of the cage and was checking the corner post when suddenly, Lady launched herself full flight from the far side of the cage. Imagine the terror that must have coursed through that canine's mind as six feet of black talons and feathers crashed into the cage wall, inches in front of his nose. Lady couldn't reach him because of a protection we had put up until our cat could get "educated," but the effect was just the same. With a hoarse yelp he catapulted backward off the point, went crashing down through the poison oak, and, from the sound of things, didn't stop until he reached the bottom of the canyon, where he spent the rest of the day barking at whatever was in the cage. From that day on, he had a healthy respect for the occupant of the "house" on the point.

There were other individuals of the area that had to be educated about Lady's presence also. Although there were houses in the area, they were all located back in the canyon away from Lady's flying area, so there was little chance that the neighbors would ever see her. However, just to be safe, Dad told them he had an eagle; if they should ever see a large bird land nearby, they were not to become alarmed.

One day, several months after we had moved in, Lady was flying along a ridge to the west of the house. Occasionally she would swoop in and land next to Dad for a moment, then launch again for the ridge where there were good updrafts. She was about five hundred feet up when it became obvious that she had spotted something. She began to pitch down then she angled steeper and disappeared behind some high chaparral. Seconds later, she swooped up rapidly, circled once and then stooped again. Often she spotted rabbits or squirrels, but she could never catch them because of the heavy brush cover. But her behavior now puzzled

Dad. She was stooping quite frequently now, and whatever her prey, it was not moving very fast and was obviously not taking to cover. After a dozen stoops, Dad decided to go up the fire break and see what she was after. It took ten minutes for him to get over the ridge, and there is no telling how many stoops she had made during that time. As Dad came to the crest of the knoll and looked down on the ridge, he was horrified. Lady was once again bearing down on her target, a white haired old gentleman who was making painfully slow progress down the trail. As Lady approached him, he stopped and waved his cane at her, yelling in a raspy voice until she pulled up; then while she was circling around for another attack, he worked his way down the trail. Dad raced down the hill yelling at Lady, trying to ward off another attack, but Lady was not to be deterred on this run. The old man once again paused and waved his cane at the big bird and she zipped on past him. Dad feared the frail old man would have a heart attack, or at least fall and break a limb. Or, even worse, the eagle might finally tire of playing with him and finish him off! But as he approached, he saw that the old man was not really alarmed. Of course he didn't know the eagle belonged to Dad; he thought it was a wild one, and he was thoroughly enjoying the attacks. "This great big bird began diving on me, he exclaimed, but all I have to do is wave my cane, and she never comes closer than a few feet; what a sight!" After Lady returned to her cage the old fellow explained that he always took his morning walk along this trail. He was surprised to learn that Lady was a tame eagle. Dad finally persuaded him to take his walks along a trail that wouldn't expose him to Lady.

In spite of these few encounters, the new home on the hill was to be an ideal area for Lady. In fact it was to be her home for the rest of her captive life, and it was here that she and we spent many happy and interesting hours.

BIT PARTS

After our first experience with moviemaking, we proceeded at a rather slow pace. The first films on Lady's training served as an opening, however, to other things. This was at a time when Disney's *True Life Adventure* series were at the height of their popularity, and dozens of amateur photographers were called full-fledged "Disney photographers" even if they only sold one foot of film. In fact, many photographers would gladly have given Disney footage just to say it was used.

We sold the first 2,000 feet of film we ever took with a movie camera to Walt Disney. Now, after years of experience, we look back at that footage, and in just thirty seconds of film time can see every mistake known to film making. Two things were in our favor. The subject matter was excellent and, most important, Disney at that time had an hour show *each day*, which required enormous amounts of material. In other words, Disney was desperate!

During the taking of that first film, it was quite a family

joke that we were working on a "Disney film!" Relatives, upon seeing us, would ask with a twinkle in their eyes, "Well, how is your Disney film coming?" Whereupon we tried to produce an intelligent answer thoroughly laced with film-making jargon that we had just read in our "How to Make Movies" book.

From our first film on, we proceeded with film making as a hobby more than anything else. But we were able to im-prove our techniques until we could take tolerable footage. Occasionally Dad would sell bits and pieces of eagle footage to someone, and the word finally spread that he had an eagle available for motion-picture work.

One of the first calls Dad received to take Lady on loca-tion was from a Disney crew working on a lion story in the Malibu Mountains near Los Angeles. They were in des-perate trouble. They had called another eagle trainer down from Idaho, and his bird had promptly disappeared. Now they were faced with being behind schedule several days and had no hope of getting the shots needed.

A deal was arranged, and Dad drove down there with Lady. At this time she was being flown only on the lure, which meant at the most she could fly only a couple of times a day. The director was so grateful to have found an eagle that he was ready to agree to anything. As it turned out, he got the necessary shots in a couple of hours, and, as a bonus, the lost eagle saw Lady, returned to the area and was re-captured.

Word of this incident spread around, and in a few months Dad received another call for a job for Lady. This call was from a friend who was a Disney producer and had made our acquaintance a year before. Jack Couffer had been Disney's top producer on wildlife films for several years and was now working on a project that was to be a pictorial adaptation of Ferde Grofe's "Grand Canyon

Suite." The film, of course, was to be shot at the Grand Canyon in Arizona. It was a film that would capture the many and varied moods of that great natural wonder, accompanying them by the descriptive musical movements of Grofe's famous work. Not a word was to be spoken. Jack explained the part Lady was to play in the film.

One of the movements of the suite is called, "On The Trail," and the film pictorializing that movement would involve several sequences of animal and bird life found along the rim of the canyon. The golden eagle is one type of creature that inhabits the rim. As Jack explained, it would be necessary for us to fly the eagle over the canyon in order to obtain the best footage. As he gave us details, we became more and more excited at the thought of our eagle soaring in majestic splendor over the great shadowed depths of the Grand Canyon, to say nothing of the fact that Lady would be seen by many audiences in CinemaScope on theater screens across the nation. Dad agreed to the generous offer of pay per day made by the producer. We made plans for the trip.

This was by far the most ambitious endeavor we had undertaken up to this time. Until now we had only flown Lady around the house or out in the desert, where there was really no place for her to go that we couldn't follow. This new project was to involve a trip of six hundred miles and flying Lady in an area where there was little possibility of retrieving her if she didn't return of her own accord. We began to put her through extensive training on the lure so that she would be dependable. As the time to leave for the location drew near, we began to have second thoughts about the trip. But these thoughts had to be ignored; too much was now dependent upon our arrival with the eagle.

It was early on the first day of April that we left for Arizona. This was before Lady matured, so April was not then her nesting time. Dad had constructed a cage that fitted neatly in the back of the station wagon. It was plywood with a couple of small windows for ventilation. Behind the station wagon we pulled a small house trailer. As we headed down the freeways of Southern California, we all took great delight in watching the stares of other motorists as they saw Lady's head poking through her cage window.

By nightfall we were out on the desert and pulled off the road to spend the night. The next morning, while Mom and Patsy were getting breakfast, Dad and I took Lady out of her cage and let her walk around for a bit on the leash. While she stood on a rock behind us, preening her feathers, we looked down on the desert highway at the few cars passing by. Most motorists roared down the black ribbon, hardly looking to the left or right, and disappeared off into the distance. But one car, as it approached, suddenly swerved erratically, and we could see that the motorist was pointing frantically at something behind us. From the expression on his face it was obvious that he couldn't see the leash attached to Lady and apparently thought· we were unaware of the huge, black bird standing just behind us. I am certain he thought we were in immediate danger of being attacked, but true to the nature of some human beings of not wanting "to get involved," sped off into the distance.

As we approached the Arizona border check station, the officer came out to greet us with the usual questions of "Do you have any citrus fruit or plants with you?" As Dad answered in the negative, the officer looked in the back at the cage, and just as he pressed his face close to the glass, a huge, taloned foot slapped at the cage window, followed by Lady's face as she peered out to see why we had stopped. The guard jumped back; he was obviously upset. "What have you got in there?" he asked in a shaky voice, but trying to sound authoritative. As Dad answered, we could see that this officer thought surely there must be something in his books about importing eagles into Arizona. He made small talk about the eagle while his mind raced to remember a statute or rule covering this situation. Finally, visibly disappointed, he waved us on through.

Toward the end of the day, we pulled off into the desert near a low mountain and decided to give Lady a chance to fly in a strange place, a sort of "shakedown" flight. She immediately launched into the air and to our dismay completely ignored the lure. After several minutes of flying, she landed atop the hill and refused to come down. She then took off and eventually landed on a hill a mile away. It was only after a long hike that Dad was finally able to retrieve her, and we felt that we very nearly had lost her. That evening we had our first serious anxiety about the prudence of flying her in the Grand Canyon.

The middle of the next day we arrived at the south rim of the canyon. Jack Couffer was there to greet us. He is a huge man, well over six feet tall, and his very size gives one a feeling of confidence. His voice of calm assurance temporarily soothed our anxieties about the project. We followed him down to the highway to the overlook point that was to be our shooting location. The park service had closed the point to the public, so we had an excellent place to park the trailer and work in privacy. We walked to the point and looked out over the canyon. It was immense. The more we looked, the more we wanted to turn and head immediately back toward home. Jack must have sensed this, for he began to speak in calm tones, assuring us that there was no hurry, and that we would certainly be taking no chances with Lady. Somewhat reassured, we agreed to give it a try and made camp. That night at dinner in the lodge we met the director Ernst Heineger, an Austrian cinematographer with a thick accent.

Heineger was obviously a talented man. He and his wife had traveled all over the world making award-winning films on various subjects. His sensitivity to beauty in nature made him well qualified to direct this film. However, like most directors, he was impatient and was anxious to proceed with the filming.

He was not too thrilled when Dad explained that we would have to wait a few days to acclimate the eagle to the area. He could not understand why we couldn't begin immediately. Jack hastened to explain the reactions of the eagle upon being introduced to a new area. Finally, with great reluctance, Heineger agreed to give us a "day or two."

The next morning we took Lady out to the point overlooking the canyon and let her perch on a rock. From this point she could see the opposite rim thirteen miles away; she could also see up and down the canyon for a hundred miles and, a mile below, the Colorado winding its way. She was literally transfixed by the view. For hours she sat on the same rock, just staring down into the canyon. She made no attempt to fly; she ignored everyone, including me, and acted almost as if she were in a trance. She scarcely noticed the swooping jays overhead scolding her. And to top it off, she completely ignored food. Wouldn't even look at it!

"Must be a little carsick from the trip," explained Dad convincingly. But we both knew that she should be over that by now. The second day was no different. Again she stared fixedly off into the canyon. A live gopher was turned loose for her, and she allowed the rodent to walk right across her feet and didn't make a move! This was incredible. Jack agreed that she was in no condition to fly right now.

That night there was a blizzard, and the next morning

Lady's cage had six inches of snow on it. When Dad took her out, she immediately began to jump around in the snow like a small child. Once again she spent the day on the rock, showing not the slightest interest in food.

By this time Dad and I had decided that the deal was off. We knew that we would be crazy to fly her in these conditions. Our problem was how to get out of it gracefully. Dad confided to Jack and proposed that we forget the whole thing—that the director owed us nothing in pay. He went on to say that it would be at least a week before we could fly Lady, and that, if we stayed, he wanted full pay for every day there, even if they didn't get a single picture of the bird. Faced with all these obstacles, we felt the director would be glad to get out of the situation at once and without paying a dime. Jack relayed our message and the next morning stood before us grinning.

"He says he will wait a month, if necessary, and will pay the price." Then Jack explained to us what he had known all the time. The more difficult the scene, the more desirable it was for this director. By stressing the difficulty in the project, we had sealed our fate. We would have to fly Lady at least once, and it might be the last we would ever see of her. But we had to do it!

While we were waiting for Lady to get ready, they resumed filming other parts of the film. Lady watched unconcernedly as the camera crew worked. Early one morning Jack brought a box containing a great horned owl and set it on the ground beneath a bush. Every time someone passed by, the owl would hiss and clack its beak in a loud popping sound, a warning to strangers. As Dad carried Lady out to the point to her usual spot, he passed the owl box. At the sound of the strange noise and indistinguishable object in the box, Lady bated in terror off the fist. Fortunately the leash was attached and she couldn't get away. But this strange, unknown object had really spooked her for this area. She refused to sit on the perch, bated constantly, and, if free, would have instantly flown to a far distant bluff.

It was disastrous! Until she got over this we knew we could never fly her. Jack tried hiding the caged owl under canvas, in the car, and behind bushes and rocks. But Lady was thoroughly spooked, and though she couldn't see the box, she was sure it was there somewhere. Even if the crate was not brought to the point in the morning, it made no difference. The fact was that it was an unseen danger that could be hiding behind any bush or rock. If we hadn't been under such pressure, the situation would have been comical: this regal bird peering behind every rock and bush, spooked into flying every time a small bird went past!

Finally we hit upon a solution that was so simple it was ridiculous. Dad had Jack bring the box to Lady, let her see that the "creature" was in the box, and then, while she watched, had Jack walk off down the road with the box until he disappeared completely from sight. A few minutes later, he returned empty-handed. Lady looked him over, glanced way down the road, and all was well! Later on, the crewmen returned the box unseen by Lady and stashed it nearby, out of her sight.

After four days of fasting, Lady finally began to show some interest in food. Once she began to eat, her appetite came back rapidly. Dad decided that now they could begin to get the close shots of her sitting on the edge of the canyon. All these shots could be taken with a small leash on her leg so there was no danger of her flying away.

The first day of shooting presented an instant problem. Lady didn't like the director. She didn't like his mannerisms and, especially, his thick accent! What irritated her most was his habit of approaching her with his hands outstretched so that the thumb and index finger of each hand formed the lower half of an imaginary camera frame. He would use this "frame" to see how she would appear to the camera, all the time uttering the words "Amazing, amazing" in his peculiar way. Several times she threatened him, but of course only Dad recognized the signs. Once, however, as Heineger passed close to her, she lunged at him—but Dad stopped her short before she could do any damage.

Finally the time came to see if she would come to the lure. With a strong line about 100 feet long on her jesses, we flew her to the lure successfully. Several more flights were made that day. Then we decided to see if she would fly across a part of the canyon without raking away. We chose a U-shaped part of the rim where she could fly from one promontory to another point across the canyon about 150 feet away.

The next day she showed eagerness at the lure, so we set up the plan. I went to one point with the lure, and Dad took Lady to the other point where he carefully coiled two hundred feet of heavy line. Then, with Lady watching, I whistled and tossed the lure. She watched eagerly for a second and then launched toward it. Her path would take her across an abyss several hundred feet deep before she reached the lure.

As she got out over the canyon, she felt the winds lift her and she turned away toward the rim of the canyon. As soon as she was over the rim, Dad stopped her with the line and retrieved her. Over and over we tried until she was successful in completing her flight to the lure.

We flew her several times thereafter between those two points before Dad announced that now we would do it without the line. The cameras were set up to record the short flight. With hearts in our throats, we called her, and she made a perfect flight. The next day several free flights were made to other picturesque points. Now the film makers had all the close fly-bys they needed. It was time to get the full shots of the eagle out over the canyon proper.

This time, instead of being called to the lure, she would be launched directly out over the canyon; after she made several circles, the lure would be put out, and, hopefully, she would come back. The cameras were checked and double-checked. We waited for the wind to cease. Soon the time was right. Dad launched her, and out she sailed, paused momentarily in full view of the lens, and then dipped down, gaining speed, and disappeared beyond the next point. We raced down a trail, hoping to see where she went, but as we rounded the bend, she wasn't in sight. She had vanished! Dad scanned the cliffs and the sky. Nothing but a raven high above him. Then he looked again, "That's no raven! There she is," he shouted, pointing skyward to the small speck nearly a thousand feet above the rim. As she had rounded the bend, she must have run into a tremendous updraft which scooped her up and deposited her in her current position. This was higher than she had ever been before. Her height added to the canyon depth put about six thousand feet of empty space below her. Her view must have been fantastic! Everyone raced back up to the rim of the canyon and to camera positions. Dad shouted to the director that he was going to call her down—he'd better get ready because it was going to be spectacular! Our hearts were again in our throats, however. How insignificant that lure must have looked to her in relation to the vastness below her! Surely she would ignore it and drift off. The lure was cast. It landed near a bush, looking pitifully small and unimportant. For a few moments we were sure she was ignoring us. Then abruptly she closed her wings and began to fall like a bomb. It seemed to take an eternity for her to cover the distance. As she grew larger, we held our breath, didn't move a muscle for fear she would be distracted. The only sound was the quiet hum of the camera as she plunged closer and closer. With a thud she hit the lure and stood proudly. Quickly Dad attached the leash, lest she take off with her food and eat it on a distant ridge.

Needless to say, we were extremely relieved to have her back. The director was thrilled with her flight performance and felt he had everything he needed for that sequence. We vowed we would never fly that bird in such a situation again.

We headed for home and anxiously awaited the day when the film was finished. The film was a beautiful work and it won an Academy Award. Lady appeared, proud and beautiful, but somehow the few minutes on the screen didn't reveal the anxious moments we had all gone through. A viewer would see only the simple beauty of a majestic eagle soaring above one of nature's wonders.

Despite the fact that we were delighted with her appearing in a film, we had not forgotten that our original purpose in capturing Lady was, as our permit stated, educational; we were carrying on scientific research. We had by now privately recorded on film the experiences of Lady's first nesting year. We had also filmed the various intelligence tests that we had given Lady and recorded many other interesting behavioral observations. This footage was put together in a short film entitled "Eagle Sense" which I used as a lecture film through Southern California. Though our film was a significant achievement, we felt that our film work with Lady had by no means ended. We were interested in the production of a great spectacular revolving around the eagle, a spectacular that would be filmed in beautiful country and utilize all the "talents" Lady possessed. Dad and I spent countless hours discussing ideas for such a film. But this kind of project required money, contacts and experience. We had little of any of these. So our great spectacular remained for now just a thought to tantalize our ego.

One day a friend who was an agent for television properties stopped by. During the course of his visit, Dad showed him "Eagle Sense." He was quite excited about it and asked to borrow the reel—he was sure he could sell it. Somewhat skeptically, Dad gave it to him, and he rushed off. Within just a few days, he called to say that he had an interested "party" that would like to buy segments of the reel. At first this just appeared to be a stock footage sale but, as he explained further, the proposition became more interesting. The client was the *Lassie* television producer; he was interested in developing a story around Lady and the goslings. The writers felt that they could easily incorporate the existing footage into an interesting show. Negotiations were begun, and soon Dad had a contract.

The script was cleverly written to include much of the gosling-eagle footage. Briefly, it was the story of a small boy who, while watching an eagle on the nest, sees an egg collector rob the nest of its only egg while the mother is away. Feeling sorry for the mother, the boy takes a goose egg from the farm barnyard and puts it into the nest. From there on the story followed the actual experience; finally, the full-grown goose is shown making his way back to the barnyard.

It was a simple story, and quite a touching one. However, there were many bird watchers across the land that were dumbfounded at what they saw. To most of them it was "another one of those Hollywood tricks," probably "done with mirrors."

That first *Lassie* show was such a success that the *Lassie* writers began to plan another for the next season. In fact, for several years one episode per season was an eagle show. In order to have a different story each time, considerable imagination had to be used. For one thing, we were limited in that Lady could only do certain things—she certainly was no Lassie. Another limitation was that Lassie always had to be the hero, and, at our insistence, Lady had to be portrayed as a member of a beneficial species. So most of the stories were alliances between the dog and Lady as they overcame a common enemy or problem.

In many of these shows Dad had to train Lady to perform a specific task. Often these were variations of previous tasks we had taught her to do. On one show the script had Lassie and her puppies in need of food; Lassie couldn't leave the puppies because a coyote was on the prowl nearby. Lady somehow "understands" the problem and flies off where she spots a campground. She sees a fisherman put some food in a campground food locker and then go off down a trail. Once he is out of sight, Lady flies down to the food locker, and scrutinizes it closely. She then opens it very cleverly, and gets some food and returns to Lassie.

During Lady's nesting period, she had a strong urge to carry things. Often while flying she would pick up twigs or green branches and sail into the nest. These things were used to "dress up" the nest a bit. In the wild, twigs and green boughs often provide shade for the youngsters. Dad soon discovered that he could induce her to take almost anything to the nest. One time he found on the firebreak an old discarded broom of unexplained origin. For the fun of it he gave it to Lady and off she went, gaining altitude. She then began the long dive back to the nest with the broom clutched neatly in her feet and held in a position to streamline the flow of air. As she swooped down from high up, she looked not unlike some prankster's version of the wicked witch on Hallowe'en. With her wings almost closed, she appeared to be riding the broom instead of carrying it!

One complicated *Lassie* show involved an old hermit who

lived high on a hill in a dilapidated shack. People around thought he was a bit crazy because he had a pet eagle that circled constantly above his mountain retreat. The old hermit died, and the eagle was now seen carrying a satchel with her constantly. She flew everywhere with the satchel dangling beneath her. Of course everyone wondered what was in it, since the eagle never let it go. To add to the mystery, there was an inscription on the wall of the old man's cabin that indicated that the eagle carried a precious cargo and that whoever was successful in getting the satchel would be greatly rewarded. But, the note warned, the eagle must not be harmed.

The script involved several "gimmicks" that required special training. For one thing, in nearly every flying scene Lady had to be carrying the satchel. There had to be take-offs with the satchel as well as landings. As has been mentioned before, Lady could be induced to carry almost anything to her nest, so this new task was just another variation. Dad began to put all her meals in the satchel. At first he just put the bag in her cage where she took the meat out and fed her youngster. The next time the bag was placed outside with the meat in it, and she retrieved the food and again fed her youngster. So it was just a matter of extending the distance she had to go to get the food. She had to learn that the satchel always contained food for her youngster. Finally, after many training sessions Dad could put the satchel up on the firebreak half a mile away and Lady would go get it. On the flight back to the cage, Dad got shots of her in many different angles carrying the satchel. In order to have her land on various perches with the bag, he simply put her baby gosling in a basket and moved him to the desired location. Lady always returned to the baby, not the cage.

In the story Timmy, the small boy of the *Lassie* show at

that time, and his friend, an elderly gentleman, tried several ways to get the satchel, but to no avail. They finally decided that they would have to prove to the big bird that they were friends. The old gentleman constructs a large kite of the design used for observation kites during the Civil War and makes it a means of contacting the eagle.

In the story, Timmy and his friend would put a piece of meat on the kite for the eagle, and as the eagle learned to feed from the kite, they would decrease the distance between themselves and the bird until the eagle finally realized they were friends. The story was somewhat unbelievable, but it nevertheless made a spectacular film. The kite sequence was probably one of the most difficult ones ever taught to Lady.

Dad began by showing her that there was a piece of meat on the kite and then allowing her to take it off while he held the kite. The first step was not an easy one, since she first had to get used to the kite. The size of the kite—it was about six feet long—and its bright colors at first frightened her. But soon feeding off the kite became a regular ritual, with the distance being slowly lengthened until Lady was flying a hundred yards to pick off the meat. But this was with the kite sitting stationary on the ground. The real problem was getting her to remove the meat from the kite when it was airborne.

One day Dad showed her the meat on the kite and then sent the kite immediately into the air. She took off and followed it up, but just didn't quite know how to cope with the thing as it bounced around on the air currents. Around and around she circled, afraid to get too close because now it almost appeared as if it were alive. Finally she landed, in complete bewilderment at this new development. Day after day she tried, each time getting closer, but at the last minute flinching away. It was a beautiful sight to see the colorful kite several hundred feet up in a stiff wind, with the eagle wheeling back and forth above it. Finally she solved the problem of approach. With wings fully opened she approached the bouncing kite in as slow a flight as she could manage without stalling. She maneuvered her wings expertly so that her body matched each movement of the kite. As she neared the meat, her feet were extended, and for a moment she hovered motionless while one foot neatly plucked off the meat. Then she dipped one wing and dropped off in a steep dive to her nest far below. It was a breathtaking sight, and as such was the climax of the film. Of course in the film she finally allowed the old man and the boy to see the satchel, and much to their disappointment, they found it contained no treasure of gold. Instead there was a note with a simple verse indicating they had now gained the greatest reward, the trust of an eagle.

Since the first show about Lady and the gosling was such a success, the writers wanted to try a variation on the theme of adoptions by Lady. Dad also wanted to try Lady with a different kind of offspring. She had, by now, raised several geese, and it was inevitable that something else be tried. A script was written in which Lady had to take over a nest of Great Horned Owls while Lassie helped the mother owl who had been injured by a marauding possum. The idea was, to be sure, an unusual one, and one not likely ever to take place in nature. Hollywood has never been noted for its authenticity in nature subjects, and this "far out" story bothered us a bit. However, the script did provide us with the opportunity to experiment further with Lady's adoption behavior and at the same time be paid to record the whole story on film. Since Dad always retained the original film, we were assured that the footage would only be used in this one *Lassie* show and that we would retain all other rights to it. So, with this in mind, preparations were made.

As has been mentioned before, Lady usually laid her first egg during the first week of March. Until she was earnestly incubating there was no chance that she would accept a substitute. The problem with this situation was that great horned owls are early nesters, usually incubating in February, and have youngsters nearly grown by the time an eagle's egg hatches. It was obvious that we could never find a great horned owl egg unhatched at the time Lady began to set. Our only possibility was to find an owlet that was quite small and hope that she would accept an "instant" baby. So the search was launched to find a very "late" great horned owl nest. In the many nests we found, the owlets were much too large to accept an eagle· as their mother. It looked as if the whole project would fail for want of a three-day-old owlet. Eventually, however, a nest was found that for some reason was extremely late, and it contained five tiny, fluffy owlets. At the sight of these cute youngsters with their oversized eyes, Dad had a wild idea. If one owlet being raised by an eagle was cute, four would be four times as cute! So, leaving the mother owl with one youngster, he carried home the four others. In the haste of the moment, he hadn't really questioned whether Lady would accept four youngsters.

From the beginning this owl experiment was different. In the first place Lady had just settled down for the pre-scribed incubation period of thirty to thirty-five days when Dad found the owls. Of course he couldn't wait until Lady's incubation period was up to give her the owls; they would be half grown by then! The whole thing had to be carried out cautiously. He didn't want to endanger the owls.

As she always did, Lady welcomed Dad into her presence and stiffly got up off her nest. By now it was obvious that she accepted him as her mate, for she would let him "in-cubate" the egg while she stretched her stiff muscles. Usually she would go out and fly for twenty or thirty minutes while he stood by with the egg under his arm, keeping it warm. This time Dad had brought with him an old empty eggshell, and while she was flying he made a switch. Carefully he placed a tiny owlet between the two halves of the shell and waited for Lady's return. Breathlessly he watched as she approached the nest. What would be her reaction to this baby so early in her incubation? He stood ready to rescue the baby if Lady appeared hostile toward it. She approached the egg cautiously, as usual, but a slight movement caused the two halves to fall apart, revealing a perfectly developed owl. For a moment she paused in mid-stride, as if trying to understand this strange phenomenon. Then she resumed her approach, leaned over and gently lifted part of the shell away and then began clucking like a mother hen! Dad thought he detected a look of relief on her face because now she didn't have to put in those endless hours of incubation! Quickly she began to feed the youngster, and since this was a bird of prey, he reacted exactly as he should. He stayed put in the nest and eagerly gobbled down everything she offered him. After raising goslings, Lady must have found this a real treat!

The next problem was how to introduce her to the other three owls. Until now she had raised only one youngster at a time. Later that day Dad again let her out to fly and repeated the process with the empty eggshell and another owlet. When she returned there were now two owls. Each time she flew that day there was another youngster in her nest when she returned. She took it all in stride and didn't seem at all confused about how four youngsters could come from one egg and after only three days of incubation! At the end of that remarkable day, Lady was in her glory, busy as could be, feeding four hungry mouths that waited impatiently for her services. That night she tucked all four youngsters beneath her breast and proudly dozed off.

In the first couple of weeks, the little fellows grew like weeds, and Dad got thousands of feet of film of Lady caring for "her young." However, as they grew older, their nocturnal habits began to develop. They found it extremely difficult to remain awake during daylight hours, except at feeding time. Toward evening Lady would settle on the nest and try to gather the four now wide-eyed youngsters around her. At first they reluctantly went to sleep for the night, but after the third week they insisted on perching at the edge of the nest in complete darkness, watching all sorts of things that were invisible to Lady. An owl's eyes are, of course, designed to see in dark, but Lady's eyes were not. Of course Lady was extremely worried by their behavior and, of necessity, she was awake all night with them. But as soon as morning arrived, the youngsters promptly dropped off to sleep, leaving their harried mother to face the day with drooping eyelids.

As the youngsters became more active, they caused Lady great concern as they clambered from perch to perch in complete darkness, and she tried to protect them. To help Lady, Dad installed a small light in the cage—a "night light"—so Lady could keep track of her nocturnal offspring. The effect of little sleep was telling on Lady, and she could often be seen catnapping during the day while her babies slumbered. After five weeks, all four owls were able to fly from one perch to the next, and they spent the greatest part of the night trying out their immature voices in a variety of squawks, squeaks, and other unidentifiable sounds, much to the irritation of Lady.

At the conclusion of filming, the young owls were allowed to fly free around the house, and for several weeks they could be seen in the evenings perched on top of Lady's

121

cage, uttering their throaty hoots. Finally, one by one, they drifted off to find their own particular niche in the environment.

Through the years there were to be many more film offers, some of which Dad flatly refused. One such offer came from a TV producer who had a script which would involve considerable flying for Lady and would no doubt have been lucrative for Dad. But the hitch came when the producer said the story was about a bald eagle (our national emblem) and, since no one had a trained bald eagle, he wanted Dad to paint the head and tail feathers of Lady white so she could impersonate a bald eagle! Aside from the fact that this was an outright deception, there was the very real fact that Lady would not stand for this kind of treatment.

Subsequent films allowed us to try Lady with even more types and numbers of offspring. One year she raised a pair of young red-tailed hawks quite happily. These young hawks were the closest thing to eaglets she had ever had. Not only did they respond to her feedings properly, but they were happy to go to sleep at a decent hour.

One spring Dad decided to try baby ducklings. He had an idea for a film, so he introduced five baby ducklings into Lady's nest while she was flying. Upon her return she promptly adopted them, and for her, another spring was underway. The ducklings were easy to imprint at this age, and soon they were following Lady everywhere. Dad even built a ramp up to the nest so they could get up there at bedtime. What a sight to see Lady bedded down with five active ducklings peeking out from under her!

The filming went slower than expected, and suddenly Dad realized these little fellows were growing out of character. It was important in the film that the youngsters stay the same size. So he did the only thing possible—he found a new batch of ducklings and made a switch with Lady. She seemed not to notice that her youngsters had suddenly reverted to being babies. This was done not one or two, but three times that spring, and for several weeks Lady's family never grew up. Visitors came from afar to watch from the living-room window as Lady took her charges for a walk. Generally she would lumber along, taking long strides at a fairly rapid pace well ahead of the ducks who would be racing after her at breakneck speed. Frequently she would stop to let them catch up. All five would come barreling in and screech to a halt at her feet, some even sitting down on her toes.

These years of television films not only made Lady well known, but provided Dad and me with valuable filming experience. In fact, it was as a result of this early experience in helping Dad with films that I was to get into the wildlife motion-picture business on a full-time basis.

A FEATURE ROLE

Visitors to the adobe house on the hill were quite common, as old and new friends stopped to see Mom and Dad and of course Lady. Frequently these visitors were former photography associates who would stop to pay their respects to Lady. It was no surprise to Dad one day to see Jack Couffer towering above him at the door.

"Hello, Ed," he said in his quiet manner. "Just stopped by on my way back to L.A.—got to see that old bird."

As they walked out to the cage, Jack casually asked if Dad had any immediate plans for Lady. Dad began to suspect that Jack's visit was less casual than it appeared.

With the eye of a photographer Jack scrutinized Lady from every angle. "I hear you can fly her just about anywhere as long as she has babies. How about the Grand Canyon?" he asked, referring to the incident years before.

"Yes," laughed Dad, "even the Grand Canyon; she is as dependable as a fine watch."

Later, in the house over a cup of coffee, Jack told my

father about a producer friend who was willing to put up the money for an unusual nature film. For years, Jack confessed, he had been pondering a way to use Lady in a film in which she could play a major part. He is an accomplished writer as well as photographer, and now he revealed the outline of this proposed film.

The setting was the beautiful Red Rock country of Arizona. The story was actually taken from an ancient Hopi Indian legend. It was the legend of their eagle dance, a dance which is still performed today, and tells how this dance originated. An Indian boy, given charge of the raising of the sacrificial eagle, releases the pet the night before the sacrificial ceremony and is exiled from the tribe as punishment. He is condemned to the wilderness for the period of one year; the sentence is as good as death. However, the youth is saved from certain death by the very eagle he has befriended. A relationship grows between the two, and the boy learns great hunting skill through the eagle. At the end of the year, the boy returns to the tribe alive, much to the surprise and suspicion of the elders. His stories of living with an eagle are laughed at until he proves to be such a great hunter that the other boys in the tribe are jealous. A conspiracy develops, and one day in the woods a group of boys grab Tutivina, as the boy is called, tie eagle feathers to his arms and body, and laughingly command him to dance. He turns their prank against them as he wheels and turns with outstretched arms. Their laughter turns to fear as the dance gets wilder, and a supernatural excitement emanates from the dancer. Finally, as legend tells it, the dancer mounts a tall cliff where an eagle joins him, and soon the dancer has vanished and only two eagles are left.

The story had all the elements necessary to make it interesting, exciting and authentic. Dad could see many ways that Lady could demonstrate her intelligence to the fullest.

Perhaps here was the chance we had so often dreamed of. With Jack as the writer and director, the film would have the professional guidance necessary to carry the story off well, and with his producer, the necessary funds to carry it to completion. Dad agreed that it was good and that he'd like to do it. But, he warned, preparations would have to be made far in advance for this project and he would have to have the last say when it came to working Lady. Jack assured him that everything would be done according to his wishes. Plans were made to film the following spring.

Since the story dealt with the Indian boy raising a young eagle to maturity, it was obvious that they would need an eaglet. Of course Lady would have to be the one to raise the eaglet, and the thought of Lady, after all these years, being able to raise a youngster of her own species was thrilling. A special permit had to be arranged through the Federal Fish and Wildlife Service, since eagles are rigidly protected and it is illegal to have one in captivity. Lady was in our possession only because she had been obtained by special State permit before the federal law was enacted in 1958. Now the process of going through the red tape was begun. The permit applied for two birds, to insure that we could alter filming and make it easier on the youngsters. Time was important because eggs were to be collected, not eaglets, and the closer they were to hatching, the safer we felt it would be to move them from the wild nest.

Red tape so cluttered the process and time was so short that in the end another idea was hit upon. In each state there are a few people who are able to get permits to collect eggs from nests. This practice was at one time widespread and has often been blamed for the diminishing of rare species. In our area Dad located a man who had a permit to take two eagle eggs a year and had been doing this for years! He explained that he used them to trade with other collectors to get desirable eggs he didn't have. The thought of all those young eagles destroyed appalled us, but now we saw a way to save those two eaglets each year. Lady laid two perfectly good eggs each year. Although not fertile, they were perfect for this man's collection. A deal was made— two of Lady's eggs for two fertile eggs. The two eggs were secured and carefully transported the hundred miles to Lady's nest and exchanged for her two eggs. This would have been a yearly thing with us, except that a few weeks later this collector was found dead at the base of a tree he was preparing to climb, the victim of an apparent heart attack.

Little did Lady know that beneath her in each of those two eggs was the viable embryo of a golden eagle. While she sat diligently on her nest, over five hundred miles away preparations were being made to receive her and the two eaglets. A location site had been selected atop a red sandstone butte that gave a commanding view of the country for miles around. In just about any direction the camera looked, there were vast panoramas of wind-swept red bluffs, towering pinnacles of stone, and flat lands covered with conifers. It was indeed eagle country.

A large cage was constructed atop the location; its wide doors provided easy access. Careful planning was necessary to select the location for various sequences within the film. Each mini-location had to be selected for good pictorial composition as well as for good flying conditions.

While the crew worked on the cage and location sites, Jack worked and reworked the script. As soon as he finished a sequence, he would send it off airmail to Dad to see if the eagle action was possible. Little by little things began to fit into their respective places. And Lady sat serenely upon the precious eggs.

A few days before the eggs were due to hatch, Dad set

up elaborate equipment for the occasion. This was one hatching he didn't want to miss. Photo lights were positioned properly; the tripod and camera were set up and covered, awaiting the eventful moment. Even a tape recorder was in readiness to record the first voice from within the eggs. Hundreds of trips were made to the cage throughout the day and night to check on the eggs. Through it all, Lady was the only one that was getting any rest. Dad could scarcely sleep for fear of missing the occasion. He knew that if he were successful it would be the first time in history that anyone had ever filmed the tender reactions of a mother eagle as a tiny eaglet chipped its way into life. It well might be the first time anyone had even witnessed such an event close up.

Few expectant fathers are ever spared the experience of a 2:00 A.M. arrival, and Dad was no exception. One egg began hatching about dusk, and at the rate it was making, Dad knew it would be a long night. In the small hours of the morning, the chick became visible within the egg as he worked. Throughout the night the camera recorded each precious step of the chick entering the world. By morning the first chick was entirely out, and the second had begun. It wasn't until that next evening, almost twenty-four hours later, that both chicks were hatched and Lady began caring for them. Dad put the camera away, sent a message to Jack in Arizona that the first critical part was over and retired for some much needed rest.

Dad insisted on at least a week before moving the eagle family the five hundred miles. He wanted to make sure the babies were strong enough, and besides, he wanted to record on film Lady's treatment of the eaglets. She had an easier time feeding these youngsters than feeding the red-tailed hawks because the eaglets were about twice the size of the hawks. They certainly weren't the most beautiful babies in the world with their oversized beaks and huge clumsy feet. But Lady couldn't have cared less! Tenderly she offered them small pieces of meat which they eagerly accepted. She did not regurgitate the food as some people have observed in eagles, but gave them fresh bits. There was a great amount of secretion from her nares and mouth that saturated the meat before each bite, however. It is possible that this fluid aids the digestive process of the eaglet.

Within a week, the youngsters were strong and robust, and Dad felt they could take the trip. Lady's cage was put in the back of the station wagon one afternoon. As soon as it was dark, Dad put Lady into the darkened cage and placed the babies in a separate box. He didn't want to take the chance that she might accidentally step on them as the car traveled. Since it was dark, she didn't seem to mind being separated from them. They drove all night and the next morning at dawn they arrived in Sedona.

Jack and the crew led them to the location, and while Dad carried Lady up the steep path, Jack carried the babies in the basket. Lady didn't like that idea at all and would have attacked Jack if Dad hadn't interceded. He put her in the cage and then asked everyone to leave the area while he put the babies in. He was certain she would accept them, but he had to be careful. It had been an upsetting night. Once the babies were laid in the nest, she softened and eagerly began to feed them a piece of meat he gave her. Quietly he left the hilltop to let her attend to her duties and to rest from the trip.

For the next couple of days they let Lady get accustomed to the new surroundings. From her lofty nest she could see miles around. Her keen eyes scanned the distant cliffs and searched the wooded valleys. She seemed to be eager to get into the air, but Dad kept her confined to the cage just to make sure she was familiar with the area. As Jack and members of the crew passed by her cage, she acted quite aggressive toward them. Dad was a bit concerned as to how she would react to them as they filmed. Each time he brought up the possibility that she might attack them, he was brushed off lightly. "We'll worry about that when the time comes," explained Jack, obviously not the least bit concerned.

The day for the first flying arrived clear and breezy, a perfect day. Puffs of clouds dressed the distant horizon, and Lady was eager to take off. The camera crew had been told to remain below at the base of the butte for these first flights, but they would shoot long shots of her coming to and from the cliff. Dad opened the cage doors and Lady stepped gracefully off the ledge. Moments later she was soaring out over the valley, gaining altitude. As she skirted along the rim of a nearby cliff, Dad brought her babies out and put them on an exterior nest he had prepared. In a few minutes she plummeted toward the cliff and executed a beautiful landing at the edge of the nest. Several times more that morning she performed, and the camera crew got beautiful footage as she wheeled and swooped far above them. After a few more flights Dad put all three birds in the cage and came down the trail to talk to the crew.

Jack was elated about her performance. "Why, it took us ten days of agony at the Grand Canyon to get what we got in a few minutes here," he announced happily. Then, more seriously, "Ed, this afternoon huge clouds will billow up over that ridge there; I'd like to get some shots as Lady swoops in from the distance, past Bell Rock, and lands right in front of the camera while the clouds are there. It'd be a fantastic shot," he concluded.

"Fine with me, but you had better be prepared for her attack," Dad cautioned.

Jack indicated that he didn't think Lady would really attack. His theory was that if he held still she'd pass on by.

They were going to use two cameras. He with one, and his right-hand man, Gary, a dozen feet away with another, would be filming the scene in order to get two different angles of the action.

"You afraid?" he asked Gary, almost tauntingly.

Gary was a tall, lanky fellow who had done everything from cowpunching to mountain climbing, a very capable man. "Well, look here," he drawled, "I've been jumped by mountain lions, been chewed on by timber wolves, and I'm not about to flinch when that overgrown turkey flies by me!"

Everyone laughed. It was true that he had a reputation for getting pictures under the worst of situations. Dad could see that nothing he could say would convince them.

The cameras were set up in the proper positions, each on a ledge near where Dad would put the babies. Dad himself set up his own camera, aimed not at where Lady would come from, but at Jack and Gary. Their laughter became a bit nervous, as they realized that Dad seriously expected something of great interest to happen in their direction. Nevertheless, they were now committed and Lady was launched. As before, she headed for the far ridge where the wind could lift her easily. When she had gained altitude, Dad carried the babies out and placed them about twenty feet in front of Jack and Gary. The stage was set. The background was a beautiful medley of rich red cliffs, dark shadows and fleecy clouds as Lady began her descent toward the cameras.

Not a word was spoken as Lady plunged down in breathtaking beauty. The only sound was the buzz of the two cameras. As she approached, it became apparent to Dad that she had spotted the photographers because, instead of checking her speed, she now was gaining. He turned on his camera as she made straight for Gary. A disciple of Jack's theory of holding still, Gary stopped the camera at the last second and froze. With a whack that was audible several hundred feet away, Lady hit him on the shoulder with such force that he was knocked off a ledge and fell ten feet to the ground. Without any attempt to appear brave now, Gary scurried beneath a rock ledge while Lady circled off. Blood gushed from his shoulder, and, as he admitted later, "She got in a good lick!" Before Lady could return, Jack too had taken refuge somewhat sheepishly beneath a ledge. The only one laughing now was Dad, as he described in full detail the beautiful footage he now had of Lady's method of education.

After this somewhat convincing display of Lady's intentions, Jack ordered shields to be made; each cameraman was to have an attendant whose job it was to ward off Lady's attacks. These shields were made of brush and saplings tied into place to form a fan-shaped device about six feet long. It was quite humorous to see these rough-and-ready grown men so concerned that their shield bearers remain close. From a distance each of them could have been an Egyptian pharaoh with an attendant shielding his regal head from the sun!

With the exception of the previously mentioned incident, filming progressed well for the first two or three days. Then what Dad had always feared the most happened: a high-flying wild eagle made a slow reconnaissance pass over the bluff while Lady was in her cage.

Jack noticed the worried expression on Dad's face as he followed the bird across the sky with binoculars. "What's up?" he queried.

"A wild eagle. She's gone now. Why didn't we see her when we were checking out this location?" Dad pounded his fists together.

"Maybe it's only a passing bird," Jack said hopefully.

"No, too much gold on it; it's a mature bird, and it's my

guess that we are smack in the middle of its territory. She'll be back, just you watch."

Sure enough, the next morning before Lady was flying, the wild eagle appeared. Flying high and slow, it reminded Dad of an enemy spy on a reconnaissance mission. Everyone watched it make a slow arc across the sky and disappear back beyond the distant bluffs. This was a serious thing. All creatures in nature have a territory they defend. Sometimes these territories are very small, only a few feet or even inches. In other cases the territory may include miles. The territory of the golden eagle can often be ten or twenty square miles, depending on the availability of food and good nesting sites. Eagles will often defend their territory against other eagles until the death of one of the combatants. So it was not without reason that all the men were gravely concerned.

It was too late to change locations now, so with great apprehension they decided to continue filming. Perhaps they could fly Lady when the wild eagle was not around. Dad knew that they were grasping at straws to suppose that another eagle could fly in this wild eagle's area without being discovered. The wild one already knew she was there and was surely watching from some distant cliff.

On Lady's next flight the first encounter was made. Lady was at a good altitude when in the 2 o'clock position the enemy appeared. It didn't take Lady long to spot her. Up she climbed, trying to gain altitude, showing absolutely no fear. Above her the wild eagle waited. There seemed to be an air of ominous confidence in the way Lady flew.

Scientists who have studied territorial behavior of birds and animals have found that there is a psychological factor involved in these fights. The defending bird is almost always at an advantage because the intruding bird is in strange territory and the intruder realizes he is in the wrong. Battles are often fought at great length, but the outcome has already been decided. We all knew that the wild eagle would never give up until we packed Lady up and left, unless for some reason Lady was the victor. This, however, was highly unlikely, since she was the intruder.

Lady gained an equal altitude, and for a while it appeared that the two eagles were compatible as they circled together. Then Lady decided to return to her nest and pitched down in a steep dive. This was a mistake. Like a bullet, the wild one gained on her, and everyone gasped as Lady executed a roll at the last instant, warding off the attack. Jack got the camera going at this turn of events. Again she climbed to altitude and again was attacked when she attempted to return to her babies. It was late afternoon and she had been in the air several hours, yet the wild one would not let her return. Only with the approach of darkness did the wild bird leave the area and let the tired Lady return to her nest.

Since Lady had flown in the afternoon, Dad decided to try her in the morning the next day in the hope that the wild eagle might be busy elsewhere in the morning. No such luck. No sooner had she gotten into the air than the wild eagle appeared. The events of the day before were repeated again. Not only was Lady's life in jeopardy, but filming had come to a groaning halt. Something had to be done.

Jack dispatched several members of the crew to locate the wild eagle's nest. After several days Gary finally found it only about five miles away. As near as he could tell there were no babies in the nest. Their next move was to try to trap the wild bird alive and release her when filming was finished. Gary put on his mountain climbing gear and began setting traps on all the high bluffs used as perches by the eagle. No luck.

Even if we had thought of leaving, Lady had no intentions

of moving out. Eagerly she begged to get out each morning, and since she seemed to be able to take care of herself, Dad again let her go. This time she seemed to be anxious, almost aggressive, as the wild bird made her appearance. The pattern was different, too. The two birds circled to gain altitude while about a half mile apart. To the casual observer it appeared that they weren't even conscious of each other's presence. Once an appropriate altitude had been gained, one bird executed a maneuver, and the other one returned the challenge. Usually these maneuverings were steep dives, pulling up sharply until stalling, and then diving again. Lady answered every challenging maneuver with one of her own. Dad realized that this was the signal between two eagles of their intention to do battle. Lady had decided to fight to the death if necessary. This was going to be a spectacle witnessed by few men, so Dad told Jack to get all the cameras ready, with the terrible thought that it might be the last footage he would ever have of Lady.

The two birds were now approaching each other cautiously, like two boxers sparring, each looking for the other's weakness. It was difficult from the ground to tell the birds apart once they had made contact. They came together with a flurry of wings and talons, tumbling over and over through the air, then suddenly broke off and began climbing again. As if by a prearranged signal, they again approached each other. As they thrashed the air with their huge wings, each one was grasping for a vital hold on the other. End-over-end they tumbled until the proximity of the ground forced them to break and climb up again. All day long this went on, and down to the helpless watchers on the ground below drifted the sounds of battle—angry screeches and the taunting, challenging calls uttered by the combatants. Occasionally small feathers drifted down, only to be plucked from midair by swallows building their nests.

Still the battle raged, and everyone felt something had to be done. "If we could only separate them for a bit, Lady could get back down," Dad thought. Then he had a wild idea: perhaps he could separate them with an airplane. The nearest airport was fifty miles away, but it was worth a try. Racing at breakneck speed on the winding roads, he arrived at the Prescott Airport. He rented a Super Cub and a few minutes later saw the familiar shape of Bell Rock below.

He began a wide circle, scanning the air for the two birds. Signals from the ground told him they had drifted to the south. He climbed higher, and then he saw the two specks still far above him in heated combat. Pushing the throttle forward, he spiraled upward. He glanced at the instruments and was amazed to see that he was at eight thousand feet elevation and that the birds were still above him! He shivered with the cold and increased his climb. Finally he was level with them and the altimeter read 10,000 feet. The birds seemed to be oblivious of the small plane as he tried to separate them by flying between them. After several tries he realized it was useless. Slowing the plane down as much as possible, he flew alongside Lady to have, he was sure, a last look at her. She didn't notice the plane at all; her eyes were intent on her adversary a half mile away. She looked tired, and Dad longed to help her, but this was a battle she must fight, and win or lose, it was the necessary way of the wild. He turned and pointed the plane toward the field, leaving the two birds to their job.

That evening she did not return. Dad fed the babies himself. Everyone knew that if it had been at all possible she would have returned to her babies. Talk was serious, and everyone was conscious of Dad's feelings. Lady had been a part of his life for ten years, and now that part seemed to be over. Some of the crew tried to brighten the atmosphere by pointing out how well she had handled herself.

It was true that she could outfly the wild eagle. She could climb faster and maneuver better in spite of the fact that she was a captive bird.

"She is fearless, too," Gary pointed out, exposing his bandaged arm. Everyone laughed.

"Well, at least Gary will have something to remember her by," another voice chimed in.

One by one they drifted off to bed, but Dad could hardly wait for dawn.

The rising sun brushed the tops of the ridges with crimson, flicked its golden fringes into dark canyons; light flowed out into the valleys. On a rock near the open door of the cage Dad sat motionless, scanning the purple and pink horizon for that familiar shape. There was little hope she would return now, but nevertheless he waited.

The sun had been up for a couple of hours now, and he was just beginning to make his way down the trail when something caught his eye. A large bird was approaching, flying quite low. At first his heart jumped, but then he saw that the wings were carried too low for an eagle and that it was flying considerably slower than eagles fly. But it came closer and suddenly he realized it was Lady and that she was flying out of sheer determination, her exhausted muscles barely able to pump her wings. With considerable effort she gained the necessary altitude to land at her nest. Her first concern upon entering the nest was her babies. She couldn't have known that Dad had fed them. Tiredly she set about the task of feeding the eaglets. Once she was through, Dad had a chance to examine her. Her breast had three holes, punched in by the talons of her adversary. Her right thigh was punctured. Feathers were broken and her feet were full of cactus quills. She was injured badly, but she was alive and home, and that was all that mattered.

For three days she remained in the cage to convalesce

from her ordeal. Each day Dad scanned the sky for the wild eagle. After three days and no appearance, it was obvious it would never return. From Lady's condition it appeared that the battle had culminated on the ground. Slowly the impact of the whole experience began to soak in. Lady, a captive all her life, had successfully done battle; she had conquered a wild eagle in order to preserve her territorial rights. The key to her success was her nest of eaglets on the cliff. They gave her the right and the incentive to pit her full strength against the wild bird. She was unaware that she was the intruder because she had her own nest on the cliff below. As far as she was concerned, the wild one had trespassed. She was not at any psychological disadvantage in the battle. It was purely a battle of strength and flying ability, which, thanks to her good care in captivity, placed her in the best position to win. We were not proud to think that our eagle killed another; instead, we hoped that the eagle survived and found a new territory. But, as far as we know, it was never seen around Bell Rock again.

Once Lady had command of the skies, she could fly at will, untormented, and filming was resumed. There were many sequences involved which required special training. A Hopi boy about ten years old played the main character in the film. Since there were many scenes in the film that required the boy and Lady together, Dad had to condition Lady to allow him near her.

In the film, after being exiled from his tribe, Tutivina wandered in the desert wilderness for days until he was completely exhausted. Finally he collapsed in a small heap with his empty water bottle at his side. Soon vultures arrived and stood patiently waiting for him to die. Just at the critical moment when one vulture was preparing to extract a sample from the motionless body, the eagle appeared high above in a screaming dive. With one swoop she scattered the vultures and landed beside the still form. Then she picked up the water bottle and flew to a distant stream, landed in the water, allowed the flask to fill, and returned to the boy. He roused enough to drink and soon was revived. From that time on the boy and the eagle were always together. There were dramatic shots of the boy high on a cliff with the eagle behind him. Often she caught wild ducks and brought them to the boy for food. There were games he invented which were variations on certain tricks that we had taught Lady. Just about everything that Lady had been taught was incorporated into the script.

By midsummer the eaglets were nearly full grown. Daily they exercised their wings atop the bluff while Lady swooped back and forth above them. She was in her glory: this was her territory, and her babies would soon be flying with her. The film was rapidly reaching completion now, and in just a few more days Dad would pack Lady and her youngsters up and head for California. The whole experience had been very rewarding. Not only had the "Legend of the Boy and the Eagle" been filmed, but Dad shot thousands of feet of rare footage of Lady and her nest in a natural setting. It was a chance that he would never have again. As he sat on the bluff near the nest and watched Lady sail in and land lightly next to her nearly grown youngsters, fuss over them a bit, and spring back into the air, he felt that perhaps now he had repaid her for all those years in captivity. But nothing could erase those captive years, and we felt sad that she had been deprived of the wild freedom in which she belonged. The film "Legend of the Boy and the Eagle" was released through Walt Disney Studios and today it is listed as one of his classics, a film not likely to be equaled in the field of motion photography.

MATURE YEARS

Even though it was midday one could scarcely see across the valley. Thick, dark clouds grew more and more dense by the minute. From down in the valley lower clouds were swept up the canyons to meet the higher ones, and soon the oak-covered slopes were wrapped in swirling mist.

As the wind grew stronger, it carried with it a mixture of oak leaves and driving rain that pelted against the sturdy adobe walls of the house. From the cozy comfort of a huge fire Dad looked out at the scene. "Looks as if we are in for another wild storm."

Mom ladled each of us a bowl of hot soup, and we sat back to enjoy the storm. I had stopped by for only a minute, but at Dad's insistence had stayed to chat a bit.

Outside in the cage Lady stood on the outer perch, facing fully the fury of the storm. "She really seems to enjoy this kind of weather. It's as if this weather brings out the wild nature in her, makes her want to be free." I could tell that he was again reflecting on life with Lady. Since the "Boy and Eagle" film he had done little filming with her. And I knew thoughts were stirring in his mind as to what would finally be her fate. She had been a captive her entire life, sixteen years, but she still had many years to go, since eagles often live thirty or forty years.

The wind grew stronger, and the large madrone tree in the front yard swayed back and forth. Occasionally strips of its thin red bark were whipped off and carried by the wind down into the canyon's mists. As we talked, we inevitably found ourselves discussing past experiences with Lady. During the past sixteen years so many interesting incidents had occurred with Lady that we could spend hours reminiscing. But always there was the nagging question of what would finally be the fate of this bird. Along with this question was the one of the justification of her captivity. A creature so wild and free in spirit belonged to the wilderness where she could meet the day-to-day challenges of survival.

When one takes a creature from the wild and domesticates it, he must accept responsibility for its wellbeing. This we knew when we got Lady as a nestling. But one question that we avoided asking ourselves at that time was often asked by visitors: "What are you finally going to do with her?" That was a good question. According to our permit she belonged to the People of the State of California, and upon termination of the permit must be placed in a zoo or returned to the wild. Fortunately we were able to renew the permit from year to year without too much difficulty— except for one year.

Until 1957 our permit was from the Bureau of Sport Fishing and Wildlife of the State of California, the fact being that the eagle was then a state-protected bird. But in 1958 a federal eagle act was passed by Congress, and the golden eagle became a federally-protected bird. Until this time renewal had been a simple process of notifying the authorities of our desire to continue work with the eagle. With the new law in effect, our permit had to come from a different department.

The new law was enacted to protect almost all of our birds of prey against hunters. Since birds of prey play a vital part in the balance of nature, the indiscriminate slaughter of thousands of hawks and eagles over the years has greatly upset that balance. Several of the more valuable or endangered species were also protected by this new law from being captured except by recognized zoos or research organizations. Since we did not fit into the category of a zoo or research center, we received a letter telling us that our bird was to be picked up to be placed in a zoo. Needless to say, total chaos hit the household. Immediately Dad called the authorities to make an appointment to plead his case. They were pleasant enough, but the law was the law, and he was told they would have to pick up the bird. They did agree to see him, however.

Word soon spread that Lady was to be put into a zoo, and a flood of offers of assistance came in. Influential individuals and organizations offered to submit written affidavits testifying to the educational and scientific value of our studies of Lady. Even the local judge instructed us on how to legally protect Lady's cage from entrance.

Hastily, Dad gathered together some reels of films, along with a research paper I had done in college on eagle behavior, and raced to Los Angeles to see the powers that be.

To a cool and skeptical audience he began to explain his reasons for wanting to keep Lady. The government's own reason for wanting Lady in a zoo were understandable. There were many eagles around the country that were being kept in dirty, inadequate cages, serving what seemed to be life sentences in prison. The department was trying to eliminate that situation. It was a good thing to do, Dad agreed.

And here he caught a glimmer of hope. They had never seen Lady; they probably thought she, too, was abused and useless. Quickly he set up the projector in the crowded office and began the film.

A lack of interest at first was understandable because the viewers figured they were in for a typical home movie show. But their disinterest didn't last long. The spectacular flying shots caught everyone's attention. At the sight of an eagle raising a gosling, office girls stopped and expressed their feelings in such terms as only a woman could use. The intelligence test brought words of amazement from the men. Soon the entire office routine had ground to a halt. To most of the group an eagle heretofore had been only a large, black bird with terrible talons that one sees sitting sullenly on a perch in a zoo.

But now they saw that beneath that overcoat of black feathers and behind those sharp talons was a proud creature of high intelligence, a creature with a capacity for being tender and loving, a creature possessing a distinct personality. As the film ended, there was not a person in the group who would have dared to think of condemning our bird to a zoo. The permit was renewed, and eventually a lifetime permit was granted, thus ending forever the threat of a zoo life for Lady. But the question of her ultimate fate was still a bothersome one.

We watched as Lady opened her wings against the storm's fury. With body in flying position, she hovered inches above her perch, flying but going nowhere. "What do you think will finally happen to her?" I asked.

Dad gazed out the window. "One of three things: some morning I'll just find her dead beneath the perch; some day she will simply fly off, and I'll never see her again; or some day while she is flying someone will shoot her." That pretty well covered it. The first was the least likely, the last the most likely. Of course he could prevent the last two from ever happening by simply never letting her fly again, but that would have been no better than a zoo life.

The ideal situation would be one where Lady could return to the wild. But for a captive and domestic creature to regain its position in nature is an almost impossible task. Birds of prey, especially, have a difficult time adjusting from a captive life to a wild one. A big problem is catching prey. One night think that an eagle or hawk is born with the knowledge of how to capture prey. Not so . Young hawks and eagles in the wild must follow the parents around for weeks, learning all the tricks of the trade. Another big problem is that a domesticated bird will unerringly turn to human beings when it is hungry. Even spring countless young hawks and eagles are captured by unqualified and unauthorized people who have good intentions. But soon the thrill wears off, and the bird gets away or in turned loose deliberately on the assumption that if it can fly it can survive. Every year many of these birds meet a tragic death as they fly down to someone's house seeking food. They are beaten by children, mauled by dogs, and shot by men. Their trust is betrayed. For this reason we could never just simply release Lady.

A very real danger in flying Lady free as we did was the possibility of a hunter's taking a shot at her. Such a large bird is a tempting target for a frustrated sportsman who hasn't gotten off a shot all day. Long ago, in our filming days, Dad had removed Lady's leather leg jesses, so that when she flew she never had the straps on her feet which might identify her as belonging to someone. He tried to minimize this danger by never flying her on weekends or holidays.

As for as most people were concerned, the real danger of losing Lady was letting her out of the cage in the first place.

The casual visitor couldn't understand why, since she could catch her own food, she didn't simply fly away. In reality, this was probably the thing least likely to happen. Eagles, like other creatures, have territories, and Lady for years had had her territory, which consisted of a few square miles around her cage. Other eagles often passed by, but they never stayed in the area for long. This was Lady's home and they knew it. And for this same reason she couldn't venture far away lest she get into her neighbor's territory. The possibility that she would just up and leave was remote, and certainly we weren't just going to turn her loose. The question of her ultimate fate seemed to be one open to speculation; we hoped it wouldn't end in tragedy.

One cannot escape having feelings of remorse at depriving a wild creature of its freedom. I can remember as a child reading a story of a wild eagle that was trapped by a lumberjack and kept chained to a stump while its mate made daily visits until the captive one died of exposure and supposedly of a broken spirit. Many heartrending stories have been written of wild creatures deprive of freedom just to satisfy man's selfishness and greed. To this day I find it difficult to visit even the nicest zoos, let alone the roadside variety.

We cannot say that Lady had a better life in captivity than she would have had in the wild . . . far from it! But we honestly feel that her captive life approached more closely a free life than that of most captive birds. We certainly don't feel that she suffered in any way. Through the years we were able to observe her in her many moods. It was easy to see when she was happy and satisfied or restless and unhappy. Many times when Dad entered her cage she would show definite signs of happiness and welcome. Often she would nibble gently on his ear or pull his hat brim with her bill. Sometimes her excitement at seeing him was so great that he actually was a bit afraid to enter the cage because she might overdo her signs of affection and leave him minus an ear!

There were other times, however, when she seemed not to notice him at all. Usually she would be on the outside perch facing the valley. Her eyes would be fixed on the far distant range of mountains, and as Dad moved close to her, he could sense that she didn't want to be disturbed. Often he would speak softly to her, and she would acknowledge with a sound barely audible to his ears. Her gaze never moved, and he had a peculiar feeling that while her body was here, her spirit was riding the currents of that far distant range. These moments seldom lasted long, and soon she would again be her old self.

For the most part we feel that Lady led an interesting and happy life in captivity. The fact that she reared young every year for twelve years is ample evidence that she was happily adjusted to this life. We feel that many things contributed to her happiness. Her physical surroundings were ideal. The cage was large and airy, and possessed all the necessities of life for her. The exterior view from the cage was a view befitting an eagle. Although she lived in the presence of people, they were never imposed upon her.

Another factor we feel was important was her relationship with people. In the absence of other eagles, it was natural that she would allow human beings to fill the vacancies in her life. Often captive creatures become so helplessly attached to human beings that they think of themselves as human. Such creatures can never be rehabilitated to the wild. Fortunately, Lady never did become so domesticated. She always retained her identity, and there was never any mistaking that she was all eagle. But nevertheless, she let certain vacant positions be temporarily filled by men.

Most creatures have two halves to their mental make-up. One half is made up of the positive feelings, which may include affection, satisfaction, companionship, tenderness, and other feelings a creature may have for its mate or its offspring, a full stomach or a comfortable sleeping spot. The other half consists of the negative feelings the creature may have toward enemies or trespassers, toward being uncomfortable or hungry—in fact, toward the presence of any undesirable condition. Obviously a situation where there are more negative feelings than positive would be undesirable. But it would be unwise to think that eliminating all the negative aspects of an eagle's life would produce an ecstatically happy bird. A chicken, perhaps, can be perfectly happy all its life as long as it has proper food and accommodations. But the eagle is not a chicken; it is an aggressive, powerful bird that needs to assert its power from time to time in order to feel that its function as predator is fulfilled.

One only needs to go to a zoo to see living examples of this. If eliminating all negative aspects of life produced happy creatures, then most zoo eagles should be happy. On the contrary, most zoo eagles I have seen have been extremely listless, their eyes lacking the sparkle of the eyes of a happy bird. For them, all the positive things, such as food, good perches, etc., have added up to one big negative feeling—boredom!

In fact, the only zoo eagle I have ever seen that looked happy was one that had just managed to catch a rat that had tried to snatch a scrap from the cage floor. That eagle stood on that squirming rat with pride, her eyes wild with the excitement of the kill. Even several hours afterward she had a different look about her. Her movements were alert and quick. When I again saw the bird several months later, she was back to the usual zoo posture.

In Lady's life the objects of her positive feelings were the comforts of life, her pride, her security, and one human being, Dad. He fulfilled her need for desired companionship and affection. To say that she had love for him would be misleading, because that is a term of man's, but whatever an eagle feels for its mate she must have felt for him. During most of the year he was just a companion to her, just as a mate would be, but during her nesting season he took on a more active part. Often he would go into her cage in early spring and make a pretense of fussing with the nesting ledge. In the wilds the male usually selects several nest sites for the female's approval. Lady usually took great interest in any work Dad did on the nest. When he brought her a pile of sticks, she always looked them over carefully to select the right one, just as a wild eagle would accept a twig from its mate.

During incubation Lady let Dad do the entire job of supplying her food, even to the extent of insisting he cut it up for her. She never left the eggs unless he was there. A wild eagle, of course, has a mate to take turns in incubation, and as described previously, Dad filled even that position.

The negative feelings in Lady's life were directed toward me. I filled the position of the enemy, intruder, or challenger. Her desire to conquer an adversary was fulfilled in me. I always fled. This cat-and-mouse game we had played over the years was one of the main factors in Lady's retaining the wild spirit that so often is lost in captive birds. It was very clearly demonstrated in her nesting behavior toward me.

As long as Dad was absent, I could approach within a few feet as she incubated. She threatened but never attacked. However, if Dad was present in the cage when I approached, she immediately left the nest to attack. This behavior puzzled us until we discovered that in the wild the female usually does the defending of the nest, but will not leave unless the male is there to take over. With this information we could see that Lady was performing as she would in the wild, but had replaced her mate with Dad and her enemy with me.

One behavior pattern always remained an unsolved mystery. As has been related earlier, Lady never held any resentment toward Dad when we had to cope her bill and talons. Even though he was the one who had to first betray her, I was the one who got the blame. In her own inexplicable way she completely blanked out his part in the whole horrible affair and laid the blame on me. Perhaps the old saying "Love is blind" could be applied here.

The wind had quieted down a little and the rain was falling steadily now. Lady had hopped down to the ground and was standing near her bathing pool. Dad and I knew what was coming next. For some unexplained reason, Lady always took a bath on the coldest and wettest days. Soon she was splashing and dipping beneath the surface as if it were a hot day. Back up on the perch, she shook herself vigorously and began the slow process of drying.

It was time for me to go now. Our talk had been interesting, but still we hadn't solved the problem of Lady's future. I knew that as long as Dad was able to manage it, Lady would have a home. Spring was approaching, and once again the nesting period would come, and Dad would play the part of an eagle. Little did he know that this spring would be his last as Lady's mate.

A COURTSHIP
IN THE AIR

Spring had arrived again. Tree swallows had taken up residence in an old oak tree down the hill. Loud raspy calls could be heard from the canyon as a nest of new crows demanded dinner. And out on the point Lady had begun her twelfth nesting year with a baby duckling.

But this year Lady behaved very differently: she simply didn't have the enthusiasm for her nesting she had had in previous years. The first indication Dad had of anything different was on one of her first flights. Normally she only stayed out a few minutes when the baby was quite small, but on this early flight she stayed out almost an hour. Most of the flight was out of sight, several miles away. When she entered the cage, she kept glancing back over the valley, and it was several minutes before she resumed her duties of motherhood. Each day these flights became longer and longer, toward the end lasting several hours, and each day she seemed to be more reluctant to take up her duties.

This went on for several days, and Dad became very

151

suspicious about Lady's behavior. One day while she was out, he scanned the sky with binoculars. There was Lady—or was it she? There were two eagles circling together high over the valley. What he had suspected was true. Lady had a boyfriend! He watched as they soared together. They were cautious of one another, yet drawn by some invisible force. Other eagles had joined her flights before, but she had always ignored them. But this was obviously different.

She began the long glide toward her eyrie. The wild eagle began to follow down but pulled up when he realized she was going to land near a human. Dad watched as Lady sailed in and landed on a stump outside the cage. Her whole being was vibrant. She called lustily to the wild male as he circled overhead and then turned reluctantly toward the cage. The male circled for some time before drifting off down the valley. Lady's eyes never left him until he disappeared, and only then did she return to her duckling.

That night Dad and Mom discussed the situation. Obviously Lady was attracted to this male and just might fly away with him. Of course Dad could keep her locked up until the wild eagle went elsewhere, but that would be cruel and selfish. Lady had served her time in captivity well, contributing much to man's understanding of eagles. She deserved to be free. The solution to the problem of Lady's future was at hand. She had indicated her intention of courtship, and although Dad had made his decision to allow the courtship to progress, the final decision would have to be Lady's.

Where the male came from we do not know. Perhaps he was a young male passing through looking for a mate, or he may have been an old male whose mate had died and who was looking for a replacement. Golden eagles often mate for life and seldom change mates unless death separates them. This was the best possible way for Lady to leave us. This male evidently knew the ropes of survival and was wary of humans. With him as her mate Lady would never be attracted to humans.

Early one morning just as dawn was flickering across the mountains, Dad was awakened by calls from the cage. They were strangely different from any he had ever heard before. Outside, he could see that the wild eagle had landed on the perch and was calling to Lady who was inside the cage. He didn't dare go outside for fear of frightening off the wild bird who must have gathered up all his courage to venture this close to a house. For over two hours the two birds "talked" to one another, and then the wild one dropped easily off the perch and out into the valley. Needless to say, Lady was very anxious to get into the air that afternoon.

Every day now, as she flew, the male joined her and they would go through the courtship ritual of swooping and diving, often calling loudly to one another. The male became bolder and even followed her back to the cage but, of course, refused to enter. No doubt he wondered just what it was in that cage that drew his beloved back each day. For Lady it was a time of frustration. Often she would stand in her cage and obviously experience a painful moment as she decided whether to go off with her lover or return to her duckling.

For Dad the experience was painful also. It was in his power to put an immediate stop to the courtship, but he couldn't do it. He found himself almost a bit jealous of the male bird. For sixteen years he had been the center of Lady's life and her provider. Now he was being replaced.

Each day now she became less and less interested in her duckling. She lived only for the visits from her suitor or for her daily flights with him. The morning of April 11 dawned clear and warm. It was a perfect spring day. From her cage Lady scanned the horizon with her powerful eyes. Far off, she could see her mate, unseen by human eyes, working along the rimrock. She was anxious to be off. In her mind she had already made her decision. She needed only to have Dad open the door.

Around noon, as was his custom, Dad opened the cage door. The wind was brisk by then—ideal flying weather. As he watched Lady drop off into the valley, Dad felt a momentary pang of regret for having let her out. He knew that at any moment she might leave. But as he watched her swell up on strong updrafts, these thoughts were lost as he marveled at the sight.

She gained altitude and drifted far off in obvious search for her mate. Several hours later, she dropped in for a brief moment, then returned to the air. Several times that afternoon she returned to the hill but paid little attention to the duckling. These visits were very brief, giving the impression that she was in a hurry and didn't have long.

It was late in the afternoon when Dad saw her for the last time. The two eagles were working along a ridge near the house. They drifted over the house at an elevation of several hundred feet and began to soar. Dad stood alone out on the point watching. They were a beautifully matched pair; Lady was the larger of the two, but the male was a fine-looking bird, quite large for a male. He handled himself with ease and confidence. As they circled, they would occasionally come within inches of each other. They were getting higher now. The late sun cast a golden tint over their plumage.

Higher and higher they climbed until they were mere specks. Then the male left the circling pattern and set a straight course for a far range of mountains. For a moment Lady remained in the circling pattern, and Dad watched expectantly for her to begin her plunge back to her home on the hill. Instead, she straightened out and began to hurry after her receding mate. Soon both of them had disappeared into the distance.

Dad stood on the bluff looking out for several minutes after the two specks had disappeared. Then he turned and began to walk slowly back toward the adobe house nestled in the oak trees. There was a touch of weariness and sadness in his footsteps. From somewhere off in the oak canyon, the call of the Gambel's quail drifted up, but it went unnoticed. As he entered the house, the warm glow of the fire flickered across his weathered face. There was unmistakable sadness in the eyes, but in the voice was a sense of happy relief. Ed Durden sat down and said, "Lady is gone."

EPILOGUE

It was natural that Dad would search for Lady—
not that he wanted to get her back, but just to satisfy his
desire to know that she was all right. The sight of any large
bird always brought out the binoculars for closer examina-
tion. A note written on the calendar on April 22 in my
mother's handwriting said, simply, "Ed still looks for Lady."

It wasn't long before rumors began to drift in of eagle
sightings from concerned people who knew of Lady's disap-
pearance. One report, in particular, sounded interesting. A
local rancher had observed in the rugged back country of his
ranch a new nesting pair of eagles. Dad found the location
and began to observe the pair from his airplane.

Lady had two white feathers on her back that always
molted in each year. If he could spot two white feathers on
the back of this nesting eagle he would have positive identification. For several days he made regular flights over the
cliffside nest trying to identify the female. Many low
passes were made over the nesting bird before he saw her in

a position that revealed two white feathers in precisely the same locations as Lady's. His heart jumped as he realized that this wild nesting eagle was indeed Lady. The whole problem of Lady's future had been solved simply and beautifully. Lady's life was just beginning.

It is regrettable that the eagle, along with countless other creatures, is fast becoming the victim of progress. The pressures of human population, the wide use of pesticides, and countless unknown effects of modern technology have brought many species to the verge of extinction in the last twenty years.

There is a very real threat especially to the survival of the golden eagle. In the last thirty years, tens of thousands of eagles have been killed by organized hunting expeditions financed by sheep and cattle ranchers of the West. Even now, although the eagle is a Federally protected bird, the slaughter continues. Poison bait and helicopters with gunners take unknown numbers. Today there are fewer than 15,000 golden eagles left in the United States. The pressure of years of persecution is telling on the species.

Unless the golden eagle is allowed to live its predatory life without man's interference it will take its place alongside the passenger pigeon. That will be man's loss, because each time a species looses its grip on life, the balance of nature is disturbed and man looses his own grip a little, too.

The years with Lady were rich years. They left us with memories of a multitude of incidents that cover a broad spectrum of emotional experiences. Each of these experiences enriched our lives immensely. They are things which we will always remember. If at some time in the future, God forbid, eagles no longer fly our skies, we can draw upon this storehouse of memories. No amount of money could have purchased these treasures. They are gifts to us and now they are also yours—Gifts of an Eagle.